Empirical Analytics of Demand Systems

Empirical Analytics of Demand Systems

by

Alan A. Powell
Monash University

Lexington Books
D.C. Heath and Company
Lexington, Massachusetts
Toronto London

Library of Congress Cataloging in Publication Data

Powell, Alan A.
Empirical analytics of demand systems.

1. Consumption (Economics)–Mathematical models. I. Title.
HB801.P66 339.4'7 73-11671
ISBN 0-669-86314-9

Published simultaneously in Canada.

Printed in the United States of America.

International Standard Book Number: 0-669-86314-9

Library of Congress Catalog Card Number: 73-11671

For Noela
and to the memory
of Flo

Table of Contents

List of Tables

Preface

During the 1960's the long tradition of theoretical work on consumer demand systems began to bear the fruit of applications. These developments were presaged a decade earlier by the empirical work of Richard Stone's Cambridge group on the linear expenditure system (discussed in Chapter 3). The year 1964 saw a landmark in empirical analytics, with the publication in *Econometrica* of Barten's "Consumer Demand Functions under Almost Additive Preferences." As applied econometricians became more facile in the use of computers, it became increasingly common in the 1960's for sets of demand equations to be estimated under prior specifications derived from utility-maximizing models of consumer behavior. Although these models were much more difficult to estimate than more traditional, loosely specified, demand models, the difficulties encountered were judged to be well worthwhile in view of the advantages gained. These were, principally, that the number of parameters declined dramatically in the models incorporating prior restrictions from demand theory, and that economic interpretation of empirical results was direct.

In Chapters 1 through 5, all of the models discussed work within a timeless utility frame. There being no scope for intertemporal trade-offs in such models, savings are always exogenous. A major advance was made in 1970 by Lluch in his intertemporal extension of the utility maximizing framework. Although Tintner had given an abstract outline of the solution method for the problem more than thirty years earlier, no empirically fruitful specializations were forthcoming until Lluch's 1973 paper on "The Extended Linear Expenditure System" in the *European Economic Review*. This major development is treated in Chapter 6.

It is not possible to survey all of the interesting and important developments in a short treatise such as this book. At one end of the spectrum of the modern development of demand models is *pure economic theory*; at the other, the *design of computing algorithms*. This book only deals with economic theory to the extent that it is needed to show how data may be transformed into a final form of a model suitable for estimation. Chapters 1 and 2 provide the essential background. As far as estimation goes, detailed accounts are given only in the realm of linear econometrics. For many of the models, nonlinear econometric methods are required; in most cases, the details of these methods are beyond the scope of this book. Nor has it been possible to survey the growing literature of attempts to test statistically the demand-theoretic specifications against less tightly constrained alternatives. And finally, it has not been possible within the confines of this book to give to consumer durables the special treatment they so obviously need.

I hope the many generous colleagues whose intellectual contributions made this work possible will forgive me if I do not try to list them all individually. My intellectual debt to Constantino Lluch, however, is too great to forbear explicit mention, as is my debt to Ross Williams for his selfless commitment of time to reading and commenting on drafts. Nor could Anita Burke's devoted hard work in typing the manuscript and Kit Chapman's help in checking cross-references go unmentioned.

Alan A. Powell,
Monash University,
Clayton, Victoria, Australia
August 1973

Empirical Analytics of Demand Systems

1 Core Results of Demand Theory

When it was first published in 1939, J. R. Hicks' *Value and Capital* made available to a wide audience Slutsky's very powerful mathematical insights into demand theory.[1] Prior to its resurrection in the 1930's by Allen and by Hicks,[2] Slutsky's remarkable contribution had lain buried since its publication in 1915 in the Italian *Giornale degli Economisti.* Whilst a rigorous recapitulation of these classical developments will not be attempted here, it will be useful to attempt a heuristic review.

1.1 The Triad

The three potentially fruitful a priori restrictions that come to us from classical demand theory can be formulated in a number of equivalent ways. In this book the triad will be itemized under the nomenclature of *additivity*, *homogeneity*, and *symmetry*.

We start with the commonplace observation that a consumer's expenditures and saving add to his disposable income:

$$m_t + s_t = y_t \tag{1.0}$$

Although it does very rough justice to durable expenditures, in a pragmatic approach to the analysis of consumption expenditures it is common to assume that the level of saving is determined independently from the problem of allocating unsaved income among possible lines of consumption. For most of this book we shall adopt this simplification (to be relaxed in Chapter 6). Thus we will view the total expenditure variable m_t as being predetermined by the savings function and by the size of disposable income, which itself is regarded as exogenous for present purposes.

Suppose that there are k distinct consumption opportunities confronting an

[1] Hicks in fact rediscovered the principal propositions of Slutsky before becoming aware of Slutsky's work.

[2] J. R. Hicks, "A Reconsideration of the Theory of Value," Part I, *Economica*, n.s. 1, no. 1 (February 1934): 52–76; R. G. D. Allen, "A Reconsideration of the Theory of Value," Part II, *Economica*, n.s. 1, no. 2 (May 1934): 196–219.

individual; let his expenditure on the ith such item in income period t be v_{it}. The *additivity* postulate does no more than state, in commonsense fashion, the following aggregation identity:

$$\sum_{i=1}^{k} v_{it} \equiv m_t \tag{1.1}$$

Homogeneity may be approached as follows: If we write the demand function for good i as

$$x_{it} = D_i(p_{1t}, p_{2t}, \ldots, p_{kt}; m_t) \tag{1.2}$$

(where x_{it} is the quantity of the ith good demanded in t), the small change Δx_i occurring as the result of small changes $\Delta p_1, \ldots, \Delta p_k$; and Δm, in prices and income[3] may be approximated by

$$\Delta x_i = \sum_{j=1}^{k} \frac{\partial x_{it}}{\partial p_{jt}} \Delta p_j + \frac{\partial x_{it}}{\partial m_t} \Delta m \tag{1.3}$$

If all prices and income were to rise by $(100c)$ percent, we would have

$$\Delta p_j = c p_{jt} \qquad \text{(for all } j\text{)} \tag{1.4a}$$

and

$$\Delta m = c m_t \qquad \text{(where } c \neq 0\text{)} \tag{1.4b}$$

Substitution from these two equations into (1.3) gives

$$\frac{\Delta x_i}{c} = \sum_{j=1}^{k} \frac{\partial x_{it}}{\partial p_{jt}} p_{jt} + \frac{\partial x_{it}}{\partial m_t} m_t \tag{1.5a}$$

Homogeneity of degree zero in prices and income, however, implies that if all prices and income change equiproportionately, no changes in consumption levels occur; i.e., $\Delta x_i \equiv 0$ for all i in (1.5a). Consequently we may write

$$\frac{-m(\partial x_i/\partial m)}{x_i} = \sum_{j=1}^{k} \frac{p_j(\partial x_i/\partial p_j)}{x_i} \tag{1.5b}$$

---

[3] Where there is no risk of confusion we will use "income" interchangeably with "total expenditure" to indicate m_t. This brings us back into line with classical terminology. (The distinction between expenditure and income, however, will become critical in Chapter 6.)

(where time subscripts have been dropped for convenience). That is,

$$E_i = -\sum_{i=1}^{k} \eta_{ij} \tag{1.5c}$$

in which E_i is the "income" (strictly, total expenditure) elasticity of good i, and the $\{\eta_{ij}\}$ are the ordinary own- and cross-price elasticities of the consumption of i with respect to the prices j ($j = 1, 2, \ldots, i, \ldots, k$). Property (1.5c) tells us that the Engel (or income) elasticity of demand for a given product has as its elementary building blocks the responsiveness of that commodity's demand to the various price stimuli. We also see that (1.5c) has a ready commonsense interpretation: raising all prices by 1 percent (with income unchanged) will have just the same impact on demand as cutting income by 1 percent (with prices unchanged).

The really novel element in the contributions of Slutsky and Hicks, however, was not in the above two properties, but in the idea of symmetry. Before introducing this concept, however, it is convenient to deal with some preparatory material.

1.2 Utility Index

Whilst arguments for homogeneity can be made (as above) without direct reference to utility maximization, the argument for symmetry cannot. We assume the existence of a scalar utility function,

$$u = f(x_1, x_2, \ldots, x_k) \tag{1.6}$$

which relates the welfare of the "representative consumer"[4] within a given accounting or planning period to the amounts consumed within the period. The utility function is assumed to be twice differentiable and concave.

1.3 Elasticity of Substitution

In the case in which only two consumption opportunities exist—i.e., when $k = 2$—the elasticity of substitution is defined by

$$\sigma_{12} = \frac{d(x_1/x_2)(\partial x_1/\partial x_2)}{d(\partial x_1/\partial x_2)(x_1/x_2)} \tag{1.7}$$

[4] The aggregation errors involved in using the convenient mythical "representative consumer" may not be as serious as critics of the theory commonly suppose. See Peter B. Dixon, "The Theory of Joint Maximization," Ph.D. thesis, Department of Economics, Harvard University, April 1972, ch. 2, especially pp. 73–95.

in which the partial derivatives are taken with the utility index u held at a constant value. An argument of R. G. D. Allen, by appealing to the (assumed) continuity properties of the utility index u, readily establishes that the elasticity of substitution is a symmetrical construct;[5] that is

$$\sigma_{12} = \sigma_{21} = \sigma \tag{1.8}$$

As we shall see below, it is possible to generalize the concept to deal with $k > 2$ without loss of symmetry.

We note that the elasticity of substitution is a measure of the curvature of the preference map and as such has nothing to do with market conditions or market prices. Following Arrow et al., in a limiting sense it can be shown that a σ value of zero implies right-angled indifference curves, whereas an indefinitely large value implies straight-line indifference curves.[6]

It is as well to keep in mind that one cannot directly observe an individual's indifference surface. The symmetry of substitution elasticities cannot be of much use in our attempts to narrow down the consumer's parameter space, therefore, unless we are able to relate observable phenomena to substitution effects. The intermediate link is the notion now discussed.

1.4 Compensated Price Changes

In order to analyse the substitution effect—that is, the movement around a given indifference surface in response to the stimulus of changing relative prices—we need the notion of a compensated price change.[7]

---

[5] R. G. D. Allen, *Mathematical Analysis for Economists* (London: Macmillan, 1938), pp. 341–342. The symmetry property is derived from the familiar mathematical proposition that

$$\partial^2 y/(\partial x\, \partial z) \equiv \partial^2 y/(\partial z\, \partial x)$$

whenever both derivatives exist.

[6] K. J. Arrow, H. B. Chenery, B. S. Minhas, and R. M. Solow, "Capital-Labor Substitution and Economic Efficiency," *Review of Economics and Statistics* 43 (August 1961): 225–250, reprinted in Arnold Zellner, Ed., *Readings in Economic Statistics and Econometrics* (Boston: Little, Brown, 1968). The argument, of course, only applies to preference maps characterized by an invariant substitution elasticity.

[7] The heuristic development of this section is probably due to Henri Theil—see his *Economics and Information Theory* (Amsterdam: North-Holland and Chicago: Rand McNally, 1967), pp. 191–192. That this development leads to correct conclusions may be verified by considering the total differential of the indirect utility function—see Arthur S. Goldberger, "Functional Form and Utility: A Review of Consumer Demand Theory," Social Systems Research Institute, University of Wisconsin, Systems Formulation, Methodology and Policy Workshop Paper 6703, October 1967, pp. 15–27.

Suppose that the jth price increases by dp_j, other prices remaining constant. If we gave the individual consumer an increment in income

$$dm = x_j \, dp_j \tag{1.9}$$

this would fully compensate for the price rise—in fact, it would overcompensate him. For although the consumer could buy the same bundle of goods as before, hence achieving the same level of utility, he would not do so in the face of the new configuration of relative prices. By adjusting to the new set of prices confronting him he can, in fact, achieve a higher level of satisfaction than was previously possible. Fortunately it can be shown that the extent of the overcompensation is of a higher order of smallness than the other incremental quantities involved; that is to say, for small enough changes dp_j, the overcompensatory part of dm can be made as small a fraction as we please, of dm as a whole, vanishing in the limit. If we concentrate on strictly marginal changes, we are therefore justified in treating (1.9) as if it were an *exact* compensation.

By (dx_i) let us denote the (incremental) change in the consumption of good i which occurs as a result of the individual adjusting to the newly efficient commodity bundle after the price change (dp_j), accompanied by the compensation (dm), has occurred. (In other words, (dx_i) shall represent the small change in the consumption of the ith good as the individual moves *around* the given indifference curve.) From our formulation (1.2) of the individual's demand curve, and using our new notation as explained above, we have

$$(dx_i) = \frac{\partial D_i}{\partial p_j} dp_j + \frac{\partial D_i}{\partial m} dm \tag{1.10}$$

and, from (1.9),

$$(dx_i) = \frac{\partial x_i}{\partial p_j} dp_j + \frac{\partial x_i}{\partial m} x_j \, dp_j \tag{1.11}$$

Recalling that these equations apply (as approximations) for finite increments (dp_j) and (dx_i), we may divide each side of (1.11) by (dp_j), and take the limit as $dp_j \to \infty$, obtaining

$$\frac{(dx_i)}{(dp_j)} = \frac{\partial x_i}{\partial p_j} + x_j \frac{\partial x_i}{\partial m} \tag{1.12}$$

which is one version of the *Fundamental Equation of Value Theory*.[8] This

[8] J. R. Hicks, *Value and Capital*, 2nd ed. (Oxford: Clarendon Press, 1946), p. 309.

derivative is termed the "income-compensated cross-price derivative." A slightly better notation for (1.12) would perhaps be[9]

$$\left.\frac{\partial x_i}{\partial p_j}\right|_{\substack{\text{Utility constant,}\\ \text{prices other than}\\ \text{th constant}}} = \left.\frac{\partial x_i}{\partial p_j}\right|_{\substack{\text{Income constant,}\\ \text{prices other than}\\ \text{th constant}}} + \left. x_j \frac{\partial x_i}{\partial m}\right|_{\substack{\text{All prices}\\ \text{constant}}} \tag{1.13}$$

Because (1.13) is cumbersome, we shall work in the notation of (1.12); we shall nonetheless try to keep clearly in mind the differing natures of these three derivatives.

1.5 Fundamental Equation of Value Theory

In this section we follow closely the classic development of the Appendix of Hicks' *Value and Capital.* In the interest of spelling out that treatment as clearly as possible, it is worthwhile to introduce some notation that differs from Hicks'. Partial derivatives in *Value and Capital* are all written as $\partial(\ )/\partial(\ )$, irrespective of whether it is the arguments $(x_1, x_2, \ldots, x_k)$ of the utility function being held constant on the one hand, or the arguments $(p_1, \ldots, p_k; m)$ of the demand function on the other.[10] Experience suggests that this leads to considerable confusion. In an attempt to keep things clear, below the notation $\delta(\ )/\delta(\ )$ is used when the variables held constant are arguments of the utility function, whilst $\partial(\ )/\partial(\ )$ is used for partial derivatives evaluated at constant values of the arguments of the demand function.

We start with the budget constraint (1.2), namely,

$$\sum_{i=1}^{k} v_{it} \equiv \sum_{i=1}^{k} p_i x_{it} \equiv m_t \tag{1.14}$$

Subject to the availability of \$$m$, the consumer wishes to allocate his purchases of this total amount among the k competing items available so as to maximize

$$u = f(x_1, x_2, \ldots, x_k) \tag{1.6}$$

[9] J. M. Henderson and R. E. Quandt, *Microeconomic Theory* (New York: McGraw Hill, 1958), p. 26.

[10] The demand function, at first sight, has $k+1$ arguments, whereas the (direct) utility function has only k. But the demand function is assumed homogeneous of degree zero—i.e., only *real* income and *relative* prices matter—consequently the demand function has effectively only k arguments.

In classical style, we first of all form the Lagrangean function

$$L(x, \lambda) = u + \lambda\left(m - \sum_{j=1}^{k} p_j x_j\right) \tag{1.15}$$

The first order condition for maximization is that the partial derivatives of (1.15) with respect to each x and with respect to the dummy variable (or Lagrange multiplier) λ should all vanish. That is, we require

$$\frac{\delta u}{\delta x_i} - \lambda p_i = 0 \qquad (i = 1, \ldots, k) \tag{1.16a}$$

$$m - \sum_{l=1}^{k} p_l x_l = 0 \tag{1.16b}$$

Next we note that the marginal utility of the ith good is some function (say g_i) of the quantities consumed; more explicitly,

$$\frac{\delta u}{\delta x_i} = g_i(x_1, \ldots, x_k) \qquad (i = 1, \ldots, k) \tag{1.17}$$

Consider now small changes $\Delta x_1, \ldots, \Delta x_k$ in commodities consumed (whatever the source may be of these changes). The total resulting change in g_i is given by the approximation

$$\Delta \frac{\delta u}{\delta x_i} \doteq \sum_{l=1}^{k} \frac{\delta g_i}{\delta x_l} \Delta x_l \tag{1.18}$$

Suppose now that the changes in the x's arise from an adjustment to a change Δp_j in the jth price, other prices and income remaining constant. Then

$$\Delta x_l \doteq \frac{\partial x_l}{\partial p_j} \Delta p_j \tag{1.19}$$

Substituting from (1.19) to (1.18), we obtain

$$\Delta \frac{\delta u}{\delta x_i} \doteq \sum_{l=1}^{k} \frac{\delta g_i}{\delta x_l} \frac{\partial x_l}{\partial p_j} \Delta p_j \tag{1.20}$$

Transposing Δp_j to LHS of (1.20), we obtain

$$\frac{\Delta(\delta u/\delta x_i)}{\Delta p_j} \doteq \sum_{l=1}^{k} \frac{\delta g_i}{\delta x_l} \frac{\partial x_l}{\partial p_j} \tag{1.21}$$

In the limit as $\Delta p_j \to 0$, this becomes

$$\frac{\partial(\delta u/\delta x_i)}{\partial p_j} = \sum_{l=1}^{k} \frac{\delta^2 u}{\delta x_i\, \delta x_l} \frac{\partial x_l}{\partial p_j} \tag{1.22}$$

Next we use (1.22) to differentiate (1.16a) partially with respect to p_j:

$$\sum_{l=1}^{k} \frac{\delta^2 u}{\delta x_i\, \delta x_l} \frac{\partial x_l}{\partial p_j} - p_i \frac{\partial \lambda}{\partial p_j} = 0 \qquad (i \neq j;\ i = 1, \ldots, k) \tag{1.23a}$$

$$\sum_{l=1}^{k} \frac{\delta^2 u}{\delta x_j\, \delta x_l} \frac{\partial x_l}{\partial p_j} - p_j \frac{\partial \lambda}{\partial p_j} = \lambda \qquad (i = j) \tag{1.23b}$$

We also partially differentiate the remaining first-order condition, (1.16b), with respect to the jth price:

$$\sum_{l=1}^{k} p_l \frac{\partial x_l}{\partial p_j} = -x_j \tag{1.23c}$$

In passing we note that λ varies with p_j (with other prices and income constant) because of the income effect of the change in the jth price.

Our aim next is to put (1.23a, b, c) into matrix notation. For compactness, we shall write

$$u_{jl} = \frac{\delta^2 u}{\delta x_j\, \delta x_l} \tag{1.24}$$

We obtain,

$$\begin{bmatrix} 0 & p_1 & p_2 & \cdots & p_k \\ p_1 & u_{11} & u_{12} & \cdots & u_{1k} \\ \vdots & \vdots & \vdots & & \vdots \\ p_j & u_{j1} & u_{j2} & \cdots & u_{jk} \\ \vdots & \vdots & \vdots & & \vdots \\ p_k & u_{k1} & u_{k2} & \cdots & u_{kk} \end{bmatrix} \begin{bmatrix} -\dfrac{\partial \lambda}{\partial p_j} \\ \dfrac{\partial x_1}{\partial p_j} \\ \vdots \\ \dfrac{\partial x_j}{\partial p_j} \\ \vdots \\ \dfrac{\partial x_k}{\partial p_j} \end{bmatrix} = \begin{bmatrix} -x_j \\ 0 \\ 0 \\ \vdots \\ \lambda \\ 0 \\ \vdots \\ 0 \end{bmatrix} \tag{1.25a}$$

Or, in a more compact notation,

$$\underset{(k+1)\times(k+1)}{V} \cdot \underset{(k+1)\times 1}{y} = \underset{(k+1)\times 1}{z} \tag{1.25b}$$

Since $U = [u_{il}]$ is definite—in this case, negative definite—we may invert V, obtaining[11]

$$y = V^{-1}z \tag{1.26}$$

Consequently, $\partial x_l/\partial p_j$ may be obtained by use of Cramer's rule as:

$$\frac{\partial x_l}{\partial p_j} = (l+1)\text{th element of } (V^{-1}z) \tag{1.27a}$$

$$= \text{inner product of } (l+1)\text{th row of } V^{-1} \text{ with } z \tag{1.27b}$$

$$= \{\text{inner product of } [(l+1)\text{th row of the adjoint of } V] \text{ with } z\}/|V| \tag{1.27c}$$

$$= \{-x_j \times [\text{1st element of the } (l+1)\text{th row of the adjoint of } V] + \lambda[(j+1)\text{th element of the } (l+1)\text{th row of the adjoint of } V\}/|V| \tag{1.27d}$$

But the $(j+1)$th element of $(l+1)$th row of the adjoint of V is just the cofactor of u_{jl} in V. Write this $C_v(u_{jl})$. Next let us examine the 1st element of the $(l+1)$th row of the adjoint of V. Obviously this element is just the cofactor of p_l in V. Write this $C_v(p_l)$. Then we have

$$\frac{\partial x_l}{\partial p_j} = \frac{-x_j C_v(p_l)}{|V|} + \frac{\lambda C_v(u_{jl})}{|V|} \tag{1.27e}$$

We now go back and differentiate (1.16a) and (1.16b) partially with respect to m. First, note that (1.18) still is valid, and gives the small change in the ith marginal utility resulting from the marginal adjustment $\{\Delta x_1, \Delta_2, \ldots, \Delta x_k\}$ in the consumer's commodity bundle. Now, however, we consider small changes whose genesis is an increment Δm in income.

$$\Delta x_l = \frac{\partial x_l}{\partial m} \Delta m \tag{1.28}$$

Substituting into (1.18), we obtain

$$\Delta \frac{\delta u}{\delta x_i} = \sum_{l=1}^{k} \frac{\delta g_i}{\delta x_l} \frac{\partial x_l}{\partial m} \Delta m \tag{1.29}$$

---

[11] The standard concavity assumptions which are usually made about the utility function guarantee that V is negative semidefinite. To simplify matters it is assumed throughout this book that V is negative definite.

Transpose Δm to the LHS of (1.29), and take the limit:

$$\frac{\partial(\delta u/\delta x_i)}{\partial m} = \sum_{l=1}^{k} \frac{\delta^2 u}{\delta x_i\, \delta x_l} \frac{\partial x_l}{\partial m} \tag{1.30}$$

Proceeding to differentiate (1.16a) and (1.16b) with respect to m, we obtain

$$\frac{\partial(\delta u/\delta x_i)}{\partial m} - p_i \frac{\partial \lambda}{\partial m} = 0 \qquad (i = 1, \ldots, k) \tag{1.31a}$$

$$1 - \sum_{l=1}^{k} p_l \frac{\partial x_l}{\partial m} = 0 \tag{1.31b}$$

After substitution of (1.30), (1.31a) becomes:

$$\sum_{l=1}^{k} \frac{\delta^2 u}{\delta x_i\, \delta x_l} \frac{\partial x_l}{\partial m} - p_i \frac{\partial \lambda}{\partial m} = 0 \tag{1.32}$$

Putting (1.31a) and (1.31b) into matrix notation yields:

$$\begin{bmatrix} 0 & p_1 & \cdots & p_k \\ p_1 & u_{11} & \cdots & u_{1k} \\ \vdots & \vdots & & \vdots \\ p_k & u_{k1} & \cdots & u_{kk} \end{bmatrix} \begin{bmatrix} -\dfrac{\partial \lambda}{\partial m} \\ \dfrac{\partial x_1}{\partial m} \\ \vdots \\ \dfrac{\partial x_k}{\partial m} \end{bmatrix} = \begin{bmatrix} 1 \\ 0 \\ 0 \\ \vdots \\ 0 \end{bmatrix} \tag{1.33}$$

Solving as before, we obtain

$$\frac{\partial x_l}{\partial m} = \{(l+1)\text{th element of } V^{-1}(1, 0, \ldots, 0)^T\}$$

$= \{$inner product of the $(l+1)$th row of the adjoint of V with $(1, 0, \ldots, 0)^T\}/|V|$

$= \{$1st element of the $(l+1)$th row of the adjoint of $V\}/|V|$

$$= \frac{C_v(p_l)}{|V|} \tag{1.34}$$

Substitute now from (1.34) into (1.27e). We obtain again the *fundamental equation of value theory*:

$$\begin{array}{ccccc} \text{total effect} & & \text{income effect} & & \text{substitution effect} \\ \dfrac{\partial x_l}{\partial p_j} & = & -x_j \dfrac{\partial x_l}{\partial m} & + & \dfrac{\lambda}{|V|} C_v(u_{jl}) \end{array} \tag{1.35}$$

Comparison of (1.35) with (1.12) establishes that the income-compensated cross-partial derivative of the consumption of the *i*th good with respect to the price of the *j*th good is

$$\frac{(dx_i)}{(dp_j)} = \frac{\lambda}{|V|} C_v(u_{ji}) \tag{1.36}$$

where the notation on the LHS of (1.36) follows (1.12). However, $|V|$ is symmetric; consequently the Slutsky symmetry property is established; i.e.,

$$\frac{(dx_i)}{(dp_j)} \equiv \frac{(dx_j)}{(dp_i)} \tag{1.37a}$$

or, to introduce a convenient shorthand,

$$\kappa_{ij} \equiv \kappa_{ji} \tag{1.37b}$$

In this shorthand, the *fundamental equation of value theory* becomes

$$\kappa_{ij} = \frac{\partial x_i}{\partial p_j} + x_j \frac{\partial x_i}{\partial m} \tag{1.38}$$

The symmetry of κ_{ij} makes available to us the restriction

$$\frac{\partial x_i}{\partial p_j} + x_j \frac{\partial x_i}{\partial m} = \frac{\partial x_j}{\partial p_i} + x_i \frac{\partial x_j}{\partial m} \tag{1.39}$$

Since the derivatives in this expression measure *market behavior* (rather than indifference surfaces), the symmetry restriction (1.39) is of great potential value in tightening the a priori specification of a demand system before its estimation.

Because some empirically oriented demand systems are formulated in terms of partial substitution elasticities, we bring to a close this discussion of the symmetry property in demand analysis with a brief look at these elasticities.

1.6 Partial Substitution Elasticities

We will need, for what follows, the Hessian $\boldsymbol{U}$ of the utility function u. Whilst $\boldsymbol{V}$ was defined in (1.25a and b) as $\boldsymbol{U}$ bordered by prices, we now introduce a matrix $\boldsymbol{W}$ which differs from $\boldsymbol{V}$ only in that the bordering prices are replaced by marginal utilities; i.e.,

$$\boldsymbol{W} = \begin{bmatrix} 0 & \dfrac{\delta u}{\delta x_1} & \cdots & \dfrac{\delta u}{\delta x_k} \\ \dfrac{\delta u}{\delta x_1} & u_{11} & \cdots & u_{1k} \\ \vdots & \vdots & & \vdots \\ \dfrac{\delta u}{\delta x_k} & u_{k1} & \cdots & u_{kk} \end{bmatrix} \tag{1.40}$$

By $C_w(\;)$ we will indicate the cofactor of ( ) in $\boldsymbol{W}$. Then the partial substitution elasticity between goods i and j is defined by[12]

$$\sigma_{ij} = \frac{C_w(u_{ij})}{x_i x_j |\boldsymbol{W}|} \sum_{l=1}^{k} x_l \frac{\delta u}{\delta x_l} \tag{1.41}$$

Note, first of all, that the symmetry of $\boldsymbol{W}$ ensures the symmetry of σ_{ij} (1.41). Whilst this definition might seem somewhat round-about, it is, nevertheless, consistent with the definition (1.7) of the ordinary elasticity of substitution in the case in which $k = 2$. One will notice that as it stands, (1.41) is defined entirely in terms of characteristics of the utility surface (which is as it should be). However, under the competitive market conditions assumed to confront the consumer, prices are given: the proportions which the various *m.u.*'s bear to each other will be in line with relative prices if the consumer is maximizing satisfaction. That is,

$$\frac{\delta u}{\delta x_i} = \lambda p_i \qquad \text{(for all } i\text{)} \tag{1.42}$$

which is just a restatement of the first-order maximization condition, (1.16a). If we multiply a single row or column of a square matrix by a constant c, the determinant of the resulting matrix is just c times the determinant of the old

---

[12] Allen, *Mathematical Analysis . . .*, op. cit., p. 504.

matrix.[13] Hence we see by substitution from (1.42) into (1.40) that

$$|W| = \lambda^2 |V| \tag{1.43}$$

Thus, by substituting (1.42) and (1.43) into definition (1.41), we obtain

$$\sigma_{ij} = \frac{C_w(u_{ij})}{x_i x_j \lambda |V|} \sum_{l=1}^{k} x_l p_l$$

$$= \frac{m C_w(u_{ij})}{x_i x_j \lambda |V|} \qquad \text{[by (1.1)]} \tag{1.44}$$

By reasoning similar to that which led to equation (1.43),

$$C_w(u_{ij}) = \lambda^2 C_v(u_{ij}) \tag{1.45}$$

Substituting from (1.45) into (1.44) gives us

$$\sigma_{ij} = \frac{m}{x_i x_j} \frac{\lambda C_v(u_{ij})}{|V|} \tag{1.46a}$$

$$= \frac{m}{x_i x_j} \frac{(dx_i)}{(dp_j)} \qquad \text{[by (1.36)]} \tag{1.46b}$$

$$= \frac{m}{p_j x_j} \cdot \frac{(dx_i)}{(dp_j)} \cdot \frac{p_j}{x_i} \tag{1.46c}$$

Denoting the average budget share, (v_j/m), of commodity j by w_j, this becomes

$$\sigma_{ij} = \frac{\varepsilon_{ij}}{w_j} \tag{1.47}$$

where ε_{ij} is the income-compensated cross-elasticity of the consumption of good i with respect to price j.

It is possible to parameterize a demand system in terms of its substitution

---

[13] See, e.g., Hugh G. Campbell, *An Introduction to Matrices, Vectors and Linear Programming* (New York: Appleton-Century-Crofts, 1965), p. 84; or R. G. D. Allen, *Mathematical Economics* (London: Macmillan, 1959), p. 401.

elasticities (if one is prepared to assume these to be constant over the relevant range of variation in quantities purchased). Whereas a general demand system without restrictions would involve k^2 price parameters giving the responses of the k goods demanded to the k prices in the system, use of classical utility maximizing theory would reduce this number to C_2^k, the unknowns being the upper triangle of a matrix with typical element σ_{ij}. The principal diagonal elements, σ_{ii}, are obtained from the homogeneity condition as[14]

$$\sigma_{ii} = -\sum_{j \neq i} \sigma_{ij} \frac{w_j}{w_i} \tag{1.48}$$

1.7 Barten's Fundamental Matrix Equation

It is convenient from the viewpoint of later chapters to introduce at this point a very powerful notation developed by Barten.[15] We start by rewriting equations (1.25a) and (1.33) together in matrix format.

$$\begin{bmatrix} 0 & p_1 & p_2 & \cdots & p_k \\ p_1 & u_{11} & u_{12} & \cdots & u_{1k} \\ \vdots & \vdots & \vdots & & \vdots \\ p_j & u_{j1} & u_{j2} & \cdots & u_{jk} \\ \vdots & \vdots & \vdots & & \vdots \\ p_k & u_{k1} & u_{k2} & \cdots & u_{kk} \end{bmatrix} \begin{bmatrix} -\dfrac{\partial \lambda}{\partial p_j} & -\dfrac{\partial \lambda}{\partial m} \\ \dfrac{\partial x_1}{\partial p_j} & \dfrac{\partial x_1}{\partial m} \\ \vdots & \vdots \\ \dfrac{\partial x_j}{\partial p_j} & \dfrac{\partial x_j}{\partial m} \\ \vdots & \vdots \\ \dfrac{\partial x_k}{\partial p_j} & \dfrac{\partial x_k}{\partial m} \end{bmatrix} = \begin{bmatrix} -x_j & 1 \\ 0 & 0 \\ 0 & 0 \\ \vdots & \vdots \\ 0 & \vdots \\ \lambda & 0 \\ 0 & \vdots \\ \vdots & \vdots \\ 0 & 0 \end{bmatrix} \tag{1.49}$$

$$(j = 1, \ldots, k)$$

In equation (1.49) there is a running subscript, j. This is an artifact of the derivation of equation (1.25a). The latter equation, it will be recalled, was

[14] It is clear that, for any i, the elasticities ε_{ij} must add to zero over j (imagine all prices rising 1 percent, but income rising 1 percent to compensate for the price rise). Use of this together with (1.47) produces (1.48).

[15] A. P. Barten, "Consumer Demand Functions Under Conditions of Almost Additive Preferences," *Econometrica* 32, no. 1–2 (January–April 1964): 1–38.

generated by differentiating the first-order maximization conditions with respect to a particular price (the jth). In the interests of tidiness, this subscript can be eliminated by defining a new $k \times k$ matrix,

$$\boldsymbol{X}_p = \begin{bmatrix} \dfrac{\partial x_1}{\partial p_1} & \dfrac{\partial x_1}{\partial p_2} & \cdots & \dfrac{\partial x_1}{\partial p_k} \\ \dfrac{\partial x_2}{\partial p_1} & \cdots & \cdots & \dfrac{\partial x_2}{\partial p_k} \\ \vdots & & & \vdots \\ \dfrac{\partial x_k}{\partial p_1} & \cdots & \cdots & \dfrac{\partial x_k}{\partial p_k} \end{bmatrix} \tag{1.50}$$

We also will need a new k-vector whose components are the derivatives of the marginal utility λ of expenditure with respect to prices, $\{p_j\}$. We write this vector as

$$\boldsymbol{\lambda}_p^T = \left(\frac{\partial \lambda}{\partial p_1}, \frac{\partial \lambda}{\partial p_2}, \ldots, \frac{\partial \lambda}{\partial p_k}\right) \tag{1.51}$$

For consistency of notation, we denote the expenditure-derivative of the marginal utility of expenditure by λ_m. That is,

$$\lambda_m = \frac{\partial \lambda}{\partial m} \tag{1.52}$$

The income derivatives of demand are also written in vector notation as

$$\boldsymbol{x}_m^T = \left(\frac{\partial x_1}{\partial m}, \frac{\partial x_2}{\partial m}, \ldots, \frac{\partial x_k}{\partial m}\right) \tag{1.53}$$

Using $\boldsymbol{p}$ and $\boldsymbol{x}$ as the k vectors on prices and quantities respectively, the set of k matrix equations represented by (1.49) can now be written more compactly as

$$\begin{bmatrix} 0 & \boldsymbol{p}^T \\ \boldsymbol{p} & \boldsymbol{U} \end{bmatrix} \begin{bmatrix} -\boldsymbol{\lambda}_p^T & -\lambda_m \\ \boldsymbol{X}_p & \boldsymbol{x}_m \end{bmatrix} = \begin{bmatrix} -\boldsymbol{x}^T & 1 \\ \lambda \boldsymbol{I}_k & \boldsymbol{0} \end{bmatrix} \tag{1.54}$$

Theil has termed this equation "the fundamental matrix equation of consumer demand theory."[16] In order to proceed we need the inverse,

$$\begin{bmatrix} 0 & \boldsymbol{p}^T \\ \boldsymbol{p} & \boldsymbol{U} \end{bmatrix}^{-1} = \begin{bmatrix} -1 & \boldsymbol{p}^T\boldsymbol{U}^{-1} \\ \boldsymbol{U}^{-1}\boldsymbol{p} & \boldsymbol{p}^T\boldsymbol{U}^{-1}\boldsymbol{p}\boldsymbol{U}^{-1} - \boldsymbol{U}^{-1}\boldsymbol{p}\boldsymbol{p}^T\boldsymbol{U}^{-1} \end{bmatrix} \div (\boldsymbol{p}^T\boldsymbol{U}^{-1}\boldsymbol{p}) \tag{1.55}$$

Premultiplication of (1.54) by (1.55) gives a solution for the income and price responses of demand, as well as for the income derivative of the marginal utility of income. The latter is seen to be

$$\lambda_m = \frac{1}{\boldsymbol{p}^T\boldsymbol{U}^{-1}\boldsymbol{p}} \tag{1.56}$$

or, in our earlier notation,

$$\frac{\partial \lambda}{\partial m} = \frac{1}{|V|} \tag{1.57}$$

The income and price derivatives obtained from the solution of (1.54) are

$$\boldsymbol{x}_m = \lambda_m \boldsymbol{U}^{-1}\boldsymbol{p} \tag{1.58}$$

and

$$\boldsymbol{X}_p = -\lambda_m \boldsymbol{U}^{-1}\boldsymbol{p}\boldsymbol{x}^T + \lambda\lambda_m(\boldsymbol{p}^T\boldsymbol{U}^{-1}\boldsymbol{p})\boldsymbol{U}^{-1} - \lambda\lambda_m\boldsymbol{U}^{-1}\boldsymbol{p}\boldsymbol{p}^T\boldsymbol{U}^{-1} \tag{1.59}$$

Substituting from (1.56) into the second term on the RHS of (1.59) simplifies this expression to

$$\boldsymbol{X}_p = -\lambda_m \boldsymbol{U}^{-1}\boldsymbol{p}\boldsymbol{x}^T + \lambda\boldsymbol{U}^{-1} - \lambda\lambda_m\boldsymbol{U}^{-1}\boldsymbol{p}\boldsymbol{p}^T\boldsymbol{U}^{-1} \tag{1.60}$$

From (1.58) we have that

$$\boldsymbol{U}^{-1}\boldsymbol{p} = (\lambda_m)^{-1}\boldsymbol{x}_m \tag{1.61}$$

---

[16] Henri Theil, *Economics and Information Theory* (Amsterdam: North Holland, 1967), pp. 189–191. Working in differentials (rather than derivatives), Barten had earlier termed the corresponding equation "the fundamental matrix equation of the theory of consumer demand in terms of partial derivatives"; see Anton P. Barten, "Theorie en Empirie van een Volledig Stelsel van Vraagvergelijkingen," Ph.D. thesis, Netherlands School of Economics, 1966, p. 17.

Substituting from (1.61) into the first and third right-hand term of (1.60) gives *the fundamental matrix equation of value theory*:[17]

$$\underset{\text{total effect}}{\underset{k\times k}{X_p}} = \underset{\text{income effect}}{-\underset{k\times 1}{x_m}\,\underset{1\times k}{x^T}} + \underset{\text{substitution effect (specific)}}{\underset{1\times 1}{\lambda}\,\underset{k\times k}{U^{-1}}} - \underset{\text{substitution effect (general)}}{\underset{1\times 1}{\frac{\lambda}{\lambda_m}}\,\underset{k\times 1}{x_m}\,\underset{1\times k}{x_m^T}} \qquad (1.62)$$

The term $(-x_m x^T)$ has as ijth element $-x_j(\partial x_i/\partial m)$, and consequently represents the *income effect* in the fundamental equation of value theory (1.35). The ijth element of X_p is $\partial x_i/\partial p_j$, which is the *total effect*. By comparison with (1.35) it follows that the substitution effects κ_{ij} are

$$\underset{k\times k}{[\kappa_{ij}]} = \lambda U^{-1} - \frac{\lambda}{\lambda_m} x_m x_m^T \qquad (1.63)$$

[17] So called because it is the matrix generalization of the equation termed "the fundamental equation of value theory" by Sir John Hicks in *Value and Capital.*

2 Separable Utility Functions

2.1 Basic Separability Definitions

Separability is a relative concept whose frame of reference is some partition of the complete set of k commodities into n exhaustive, mutually exclusive subsets.[1] Let these contain respectively $k_1, k_2, \ldots, k_n$ commodities, with $k_1 + k_2 + \cdots + k_n = k$. The importance of the concept for this book lies in the restrictions it implies among the parameters of demand functions. From the viewpoint of applied econometric analysis, these restrictions amount to a reduction in the dimension of the parameter space in which estimation has to be carried out.

2.1.1 Block Additivity

Consider a particular partition of the k available commodities. Let $\boldsymbol{x}$ be the k vector of quantities consumed (i.e., the commodity bundle). A utility function $u(\boldsymbol{x})$ is called *strongly separable* (or *block additive*) with respect to the partition under consideration, provided the marginal rate of substitution between any two commodities from different subsets (*viz.*, *blocks*) is independent of the quantities consumed outside of the two subsets from which the two commodities come. If K is the complete set of k commodities, and $K_1, \ldots, K_n$ are the n subsets of the partition, strong separability is said to pertain if, for every choice of a pair of subsets $\{K_s, K_r\}$,

$$\frac{\partial(\partial x_i/\partial x_j \mid u = \text{constant})}{\partial x_l} = 0 \tag{2.1}$$

for all i belonging to K_s, j belonging to K_r (with $s \neq r$), and for any l belonging to neither K_s nor K_r. Goldman and Uzawa demonstrate that whenever $n > 2$, this definition is equivalent to placing the following restriction on the form

[1] The treatment here follows S. M. Goldman and H. Uzawa, "A Note on Separability in Demand Analysis," *Econometrica* 32, no. 3 (July 1964): 387–398; and Robert A. Pollak, "Conditional Demand Functions and the Implications of Separable Utility," *Southern Economic Journal* 37, no. 4 (April 1971): 423–433.

of the utility function[2]

$$u(x) = f(u^1(x_1)+u^2(x_2)+\cdots+u^n(x_n)) \tag{2.2}$$

in which f is a monotonic increasing function of one variable, whilst the u^i $(i=1,\ldots,n)$ are scalar functions of the quantity vectors x_i in the corresponding subsets of the partition. But this is just the definition of *block additivity* elucidated by Pollak,[3] and from this point on we shall adhere to Pollak's terminology. It is also shown by Goldman and Uzawa that if the utility function u is strictly quasi-concave[4] and the number of commodities k exceeds 2, then it is block additive with respect to the partition in question if and only if, for every commodity pair $\{i, j\}$ chosen from *different* blocks,

$$\kappa_{ij}(x) = \kappa(x)\frac{\partial x_i}{\partial m}\frac{\partial x_j}{\partial m} \tag{2.3}$$

in which κ_{ij} is the income compensated (i.e., Slutsky) derivative of consumption of i with respect to price of j (and is written explicitly as a function of x); where m is total expenditure; and where $\kappa(x)$ is a function that is independent of the choice of i and j.

Another implication of equation (2.2) is that block additivity is a property that remains invariant under aggregation of blocks into larger blocks.

Equation (2.3) is of enormous potential for the estimation of demand systems. This is because it provides a vehicle for expression of many of the price effects of a demand model in terms of the k income derivatives plus one additional function, κ. In many applications these k Engel derivatives and the function κ are reduced to constants to become $(k+1)$ of the parameters of a complete system (see Section 2.2 below).

Since the behavioral relationships generated by a utility index u are the same as those generated by any monotonic transformation thereof, a valid representation of (2.2) would be

$$u^*(x) = \sum_{s=1}^{n} u^s(x_s) \tag{2.4}$$

---

[2] Pollak, op. cit., Theorem 1, p. 389.

[3] Pollak, op. cit., p. 428. Henri Theil, *Economics and Information Theory* (Amsterdam: North–Holland, 1967), p. 199, gives a similar definition of *block independent preferences*—only the monotonic function f is eliminated. Since validly we might equally well have chosen $u^* = f^{-1}(u)$ as our utility index, the difference is conventional, not substantive.

[4] For a discussion of concavity, see, e.g., Michael D. Intriligator, *Mathematical Optimization and Economic Theory* (Englewood Cliffs, N.J.: 1971), pp. 460–464.

in which $u^* \equiv f^{-1}(u)$. In terms of this new utility index the marginal utility of any good (good number j, say) is the partial derivative u_j^s of the function u^s with respect to x_j. From (2.4) we see immediately that u_j^s could be nonzero only if j belonged to the sth preference block. It is clear that u_j^s is a function that has just the same arguments as u^s itself; namely, the quantities contained within the vector $\boldsymbol{x}_s$. Thus if i belongs to some block other than s (say, block r), the derivative of u_j^s with respect to x_i is necessarily zero. That is, the Hessian of u^* is block diagonal of the form

$$\boldsymbol{U}^* = \begin{bmatrix} \boldsymbol{U}_1 & \mathbf{0} & \mathbf{0} & \cdots & \mathbf{0} \\ \mathbf{0} & \boldsymbol{U}_2 & \mathbf{0} & \cdots & \mathbf{0} \\ \vdots & & & & \\ \mathbf{0} & \mathbf{0} & \mathbf{0} & \cdots & \boldsymbol{U}_n \end{bmatrix} \tag{2.5}$$

2.1.2 Directly Additive Preferences

A special case of block additivity is the one in which each of the subsets $K_1, \ldots, K_n$ of the partition contains exactly one good (and $n \equiv k$). If the utility function is block additive with respect to this partition, we say that the utility function is *directly additive*,[5] in which case each block $\boldsymbol{U}_s$ within (2.5) contains a single scalar element, and $\boldsymbol{U}^*$ is a diagonal matrix.

2.1.3 The Utility Tree

A utility function u is said to be weakly separable with respect to a partition of the commodity space if the marginal rate of substitution between any two goods i and j from within the same subset K_s is independent of the quantities of commodities consumed from other subsets K_r ($r = 1, \ldots, n$; $r \neq s$). That is, we have a weakly separable utility function provided

$$\frac{\partial(\partial x_i/\partial x_j \mid u = \text{constant})}{\partial x_l} = 0 \tag{1.6}$$

whenever i and j both belong to K_s and l does not; and the statement is true for all pairs (i, j) within K_s, and for all $s = 1, \ldots, n$. Weak separability can be shown to be equivalent to Strotz' concept of a utility tree and (2.6) is in fact the definition adopted by Pollak in his expository treatment of the subject.[6]

---

[5] In Section 2.2.1 it is proved that direct additivity implies (2.3).

[6] See Goldman and Uzawa, op. cit., Theorem 2; and Pollak, op. cit., p. 426.

Goldman and Uzawa show that (2.6) implies that the utility function must be capable of representation as

$$u(\boldsymbol{x}) = f(u^1(\boldsymbol{x}_1), u^2(\boldsymbol{x}_2), \ldots, u^n(\boldsymbol{x}_n)) \tag{2.7}$$

where f is a scalar function of n variables, and each u^s is a scalar function of the k_s quantities contained in $\boldsymbol{x}_s$ only. Comparing (2.7) with (2.2) we see that block additivity is a special case of a utility tree.

Goldman and Uzawa have proved that, in the case of a strictly concave utility function, the above definition of a utility tree is equivalent to the following restriction on the Slutsky terms:[7]

$$\kappa_{ij} = \kappa^{sr}(\boldsymbol{x}) \frac{\partial x_i}{\partial m} \frac{\partial x_j}{\partial m} \tag{2.8}$$

for all i, j, such that i belongs to the sth subset K_s, j belongs to some *different* subset K_r, for all choices of s and r. In (2.8) the functions κ^{sr} are defined for all $s \neq r$.

2.1.4 Pearce Separability

A utility function is *Pearce separable* with respect to the partition in question if the marginal rate of substitution between any two commodities belonging to the same subset is independent of the consumption levels of all other commodities (including other commodities within the *same* subset).[8] If, as before, $K_1, \ldots, K_n$ are the subsets of the partition, Pearce separability is said to pertain provided that

$$\frac{\partial(\partial x_i/\partial x_j \mid u = \text{constant})}{\partial x_l} = 0 \tag{2.9}$$

for all pairs (i, j) belonging to the same subset K_s (and all $s = 1, 2, \ldots, n$), for all l other than $l = i, j$. The restriction on the Slutsky derivative as derived by Goldman and Uzawa in this case differs from the utility tree case only in that (2.8) must hold also for the case $s = r$ in which the goods i and j come from the same subset.[9]

---

[7] Goldman and Uzawa, op. cit., Theorem 5.

[8] I. F. Pearce, "An Exact Method of Consumer Demand Analysis," *Econometrica* 29, no. 4 (October 1961): 499–516; *A Contribution to Demand Analysis* (Oxford: Oxford University Press, 1964).

[9] Op. cit., Theorem 6.

2.1.5 *Indirect Additivity*

This concept is associated with the name of Heindrik Houthakker.[10] We recall that as a consequence of the utility maximizing procedure envisaged in Chapter 1 there will exist (under the assumptions there made) a uniquely optimal commodity bundle $\boldsymbol{x}^*$ associated with a given vector of prices $\boldsymbol{p}$ and given nominal total expenditure (or "income"), m. The relationship between $\boldsymbol{x}^*$ and $(\boldsymbol{p}, m)$ is the set of demand functions

$$\boldsymbol{x}^* = \boldsymbol{x}^*(\boldsymbol{p}, m) \tag{2.10}$$

characterizing the representative consumer's behavior. The utility levels associated with optimal behavior are

$$\begin{aligned} u^* &= u(\boldsymbol{x}^*) = u(\boldsymbol{x}^*(\boldsymbol{p}, m)) \\ &= g(\boldsymbol{p}, m) \qquad \text{(say)} \end{aligned} \tag{2.11}$$

The function relating utility derived by an optimally allocating consumer to his total expenditure and the set of prices confronting him is termed the *indirect utility function.* Since g is homogeneous of degree zero in prices and nominal income, we may reduce the number of arguments from $(k+1)$ to k. That is, we may define a new function $g°(\ )$ by

$$\begin{aligned} u^* &= g(p_1/m, p_2/m, \ldots, p_k/m; 1) \\ &= g°(y_1, y_2, \ldots, y_k) \qquad \text{(say)} \end{aligned} \tag{2.12}$$

It is, in principle, a matter of indifference to us whether the arguments of u^* are written as y_i or $(y_i)^{-1}$. An alternative representation of u^*, therefore, is

$$u^* = g^*(z_1, z_2, \ldots, z_k) \tag{2.13a}$$

where

$$z_i \equiv \frac{m}{p_i} \qquad (i = 1, \ldots, k) \tag{2.13b}$$

in which g^* is defined by

$$g^*(a, b, c, \ldots) \equiv g°(a^{-1}, b^{-1}, c^{-1}, \ldots) \tag{2.13c}$$

---

[10] H. S. Houthakker, "Additive Preferences," *Econometrica* 28, no. 2 (April 1960): 244–257.

The utility function $u(\ )$ is said to be *indirectly additive* if and only if g^* is subject to an additive decomposition; i.e., if and only if

$$\begin{aligned} u^* &= g^*(z_1, z_2, \ldots, z_k) \\ &= g_1^*(z_1) + g_2^*(z_2) + \cdots + g_k^*(z_k) \end{aligned} \tag{2.14}$$

Since the z_i ($\equiv m/p_i$) are the vertices of the consumer's budget constraint in the commodity space, the notion of indirectly additive preferences is that the utility derived by an optimizing consumer is additive in functions of the individual maximum quantities of each item purchasable with the given budget.

2.2 Houthakker's Directly Additive Preferences

In the estimation of sets of demand equations, it often comes about that we have stronger evidence on the magnitudes of the income elasticities than is available on the price responses. To take an extreme example, consider the case in which the data consist of a cross-sectional budget study. Since all consumers pay the same market prices, from the sample evidence nothing can be inferred about their price responsiveness. With many time-series the position is little better. For although movements in prices do occur over time, they very often occur together for most commodities. Thus there may be little movement in relative prices—again inference about price responsiveness becomes difficult. The problem was recognized as early as 1910 by A. C. Pigou who developed a method for determining numerical values of price elasticities of demand on the basis of *income* responses.[11]

At first this seems quite surprising. In his classic paper of 1960, however, Houthakker demonstrates that maximization of a directly additive utility function leads to substitution effects which are directly proportional to the products of the income derivatives of consumption of the two commodities involved.[12] The constant of proportionality is the same irrespective of the pair of commodities considered. We derive this relationship below. As has been

[11] A. C. Pigou, "A Method of Determining the Numerical Value of Elasticities of Demand," *Economic Journal* 20 (1910): 636–640. Some improvements were suggested in 1935 by Milton Friedman, in "Professor Pigou's Method for Measuring Elasticities of Demand from Budgetary Data," *Quarterly Journal of Economics* 50 (1935): 151–163. A fully rigorous treatment from the view-point of utility maximization theory, however, had to await Houthakker's paper cited above.

[12] Houthakker, op. cit.

previously remarked, this result is of enormous potential power in empirical applications. Effectively it means that all of the k^2 price coefficients of the model can be replaced by a single constant. Thus, we are enabled to map the linear expenditure system to be discussed in Chapter 3 from a parameter space of order $k(k+1)$ into a space of order $(k+1)$. The price we pay for this is a rather highly restricted functional form which the utility function must be assumed to satisfy. Its restrictiveness notwithstanding, this *directly additive* form of the utility function is plausible in many applications (especially those involving rather broad aggregates).

2.2.1 Basic Theorem on Additive Preferences

We start, as in Chapter 1, with the budget constraint

$$\sum_{i=1}^{k} p_i x_i \equiv m \tag{2.15}$$

In line with our discussion in Section 2.1.2 above, the utility function is assumed to be such that some monotonic transform of it may be written as a sum of partial utility functions each having the consumption level of one commodity as its only argument.[13] That is, we assume the utility function ϕ is of the form

$$\phi = \phi_1(x_1) + \phi_2(x_2) + \cdots + \phi_k(x_k) \tag{2.16}$$

As in (1.15), we set up the Lagrangean,

$$L(\mathbf{x}, \lambda) = \phi + \lambda\left(m - \sum_{j=1}^{k} p_j x_j\right) \tag{2.17}$$

We differentiate this with respect to the ith consumption level, obtaining

$$\phi_i' = \frac{\partial \phi}{\partial x_i} = \lambda p_i \tag{2.18}$$

where the Lagrangean multiplier λ may be interpreted as the marginal utility

[13] The derivation which follows does no more than spell out Houthakker's rather concise derivation in his article, "Additive Preferences," op. cit.

of income.[14] Next, we differentiate (2.18) with respect to income, obtaining

$$\phi_i'' \frac{\partial x_i}{\partial m} = p_i \frac{\partial \lambda}{\partial m} \tag{2.19}$$

where $\phi_i'' = \partial^2 \phi / \partial x_i^2$. We also differentiate the budget equation with respect to m:

$$\sum_{i=1}^{k} p_i \frac{\partial x_i}{\partial m} = 1 \tag{2.20}$$

Choose an arbitrary commodity l, and differentiate the first-order condition (2.18) with respect to the price of that commodity:

$$\phi_i'' \frac{\partial x_i}{\partial p_l} = p_i \frac{\partial \lambda}{\partial p_l} \qquad (l \text{ different from } i) \tag{2.21}$$

$$\phi_l'' \frac{\partial x_l}{\partial p_l} = p_l \frac{\partial \lambda}{\partial p_l} + \lambda \qquad (\text{when } l = i) \tag{2.22}$$

(Above, the marginal utility of income may be assumed to have nonzero partial derivatives with respect to prices in view of the income effects of the price changes.)

Finally, we differentiate the budget equation with respect to the jth price, obtaining

$$\frac{\partial}{\partial p_j}\left(\sum_{i \neq j} p_i x_i + p_j x_j - m\right) = 0$$

$$\sum_{i \neq j} p_i \frac{\partial x_i}{\partial p_j} + p_j \frac{\partial x_j}{\partial p_j} + x_j = 0$$

$$\sum_{i=1}^{k} p_i \frac{\partial x_i}{\partial p_j} = -x_j \tag{2.23}$$

---

[14] In any Lagrangean problem the value of the Lagrangean multiplier may be interpreted as the marginal pay-off in the objective function if, at a constrained optimum position, the constraint corresponding to that multiplier is relaxed by a marginal unit. See, e.g., C. E. Ferguson, *The Neoclassical Theory of Production and Distribution* (Cambridge University Press, 1969), pp. 157–158.

Solve (2.19) for $\partial x_i/\partial m$, and substitute into (2.20):

$$\sum_{i=1}^{k} p_i \frac{\partial x_i}{\partial m} = \sum_{i=1}^{k} p_i \frac{p_i\, \partial\lambda/\partial m}{\phi_i''}$$

$$= \frac{\partial\lambda}{\partial m} \sum_{i=1}^{k} \frac{p_i^2}{\phi_i''}$$

$$= 1$$

which is the RHS of (2.20). So,

$$\frac{\partial\lambda}{\partial m} = 1 \div \left(\sum_{i=1}^{k} \frac{p_i^2}{\phi_i''} \right) \tag{2.24}$$

Next, rewrite the LHS of (2.23) as:

$$\sum_{i=1}^{k} p_i \frac{\partial x_i}{\partial p_j} = \sum_{i \neq j} p_i \frac{\partial x_i}{\partial p_j} + p_j \frac{\partial x_j}{\partial p_j}$$

Into the above, substitute for $\partial x_i/\partial p_j$ and $\partial x_j/\partial p_j$ the expressions obtained by solving (2.21) and (2.22):

$$\sum_{i=1}^{k} p_i \frac{\partial x_i}{\partial p_j} = \sum_{i \neq j} p_i \left(\frac{\partial\lambda}{\partial p_j} \frac{p_i}{\phi_i''} \right) + p_j \left(\frac{\partial\lambda}{\partial p_j} \frac{p_j}{\phi_j''} + \frac{\lambda}{\phi_j''} \right)$$

$$= \sum_{i=1}^{k} \frac{p_i^2}{\phi_i''} \frac{\partial\lambda}{\partial p_j} + p_j \frac{\lambda}{\phi_j''}$$

$$= \frac{\partial\lambda}{\partial p_j} \sum_{i=1}^{k} \frac{p_i^2}{\phi_i''} + p_j \frac{\lambda}{\phi_j''}$$

$$= -x_j \tag{2.25}$$

which is the RHS of (2.23). Rearranging (2.25), we obtain the following expression for the derivative of the marginal utility of income with respect to the *j*th price:

$$\frac{\partial\lambda}{\partial p_j} = -\left(x_j + p_j \frac{\lambda}{\phi_j''} \right) \div \left(\sum_{i=1}^{k} \frac{p_i^2}{\phi_i''} \right) \tag{2.26}$$

Notice from (2.19) that

$$p_j \frac{\lambda}{\phi_j''} = \lambda \frac{\partial x_j/\partial m}{\partial \lambda/\partial m} \tag{2.27}$$

The ratio of the marginal utility of income to this marginal utility's derivative with respect to income is, by definition

$$\psi = \frac{\lambda}{\partial \lambda/\partial m} \tag{2.28}$$

Hence we can rewrite (2.27) as

$$p_j \frac{\lambda}{\phi_j''} = \psi \frac{\partial x_j}{\partial m} \tag{2.29}$$

Dividing (2.26) by (2.24), we obtain

$$\frac{\partial \lambda/\partial p_j}{\partial \lambda/\partial m} = -\left(x_j + p_j \frac{\lambda}{\phi_j''}\right) \tag{2.30}$$

We now substitute from (2.29) into the RHS of (2.30), obtaining

$$\frac{\partial \lambda/\partial p_j}{\partial \lambda/\partial m} = -\left(x_j + \psi \frac{\partial x_j}{\partial m}\right) \tag{2.31}$$

or equivalently

$$\frac{\partial \lambda}{\partial p_j} = -\frac{\partial \lambda}{\partial m}\left(x_j + \psi \frac{\partial x_j}{\partial m}\right) \tag{2.32}$$

Now, from (2.21),

$$\frac{\partial \lambda}{\partial p_j} = \frac{\partial x_i}{\partial p_j} \frac{\phi_i''}{p_i} \qquad \text{(where } i \neq j\text{)} \tag{2.33}$$

Equating (2.32) with (2.33), and solving for $\partial x_i/\partial p_j$, we obtain

$$\frac{\partial x_i}{\partial p_j} = -x_j \frac{p_i(\partial \lambda/\partial m)}{\phi_i''} - \psi \frac{\partial \lambda}{\partial m} \frac{\partial x_j}{\partial m} \frac{p_i}{\phi_i''} \tag{2.34}$$

$$= -\frac{p_i(\partial \lambda/\partial m)}{\phi_i''}\left\{x_j + \psi \frac{\partial x_j}{\partial m}\right\} \tag{2.35}$$

From (2.19) we see that

$$\frac{p_i(\partial\lambda/\partial m)}{\phi_i''} = \frac{\partial x_i}{\partial m} \qquad (2.36)$$

Substituting this expression into the RHS of (2.35), we obtain

$$\frac{\partial x_i}{\partial p_j} = -\frac{\partial x_i}{\partial m}\left\{x_j + \psi\frac{\partial x_j}{\partial m}\right\} \qquad (2.37)$$

Equation (2.37) can immediately be identified with the *fundamental equation of value theory*, from which it differs in one term only. Recall that this fundamental equation, (1.12), is

$$\frac{(dx_i)}{(dp_j)} = \frac{\partial x_i}{\partial p_j} + x_j\frac{\partial x_i}{\partial m} \qquad (i \neq j) \qquad (2.38)$$

where $(d*)/(d**)$, as before, indicates the compensated consumption derivative of $(*)$ with respect to $(**)$. Substitute for the uncompensated derivative $(\partial x_i/\partial p_j)$ from (2.37) into the RHS of (2.38):

$$\kappa_{ij} = \frac{(dx_i)}{(dp_j)} = -\psi\frac{\partial x_i}{\partial m}\frac{\partial x_j}{\partial m} \qquad (i \neq j) \qquad (2.39)$$

which is a special case of (2.3). In words: "Under directly additive preferences, compensated cross-substitution effects are directly proportional to income derivatives." This is Houthakker's result on directly additive preferences.

2.2.2 Stone-Geary Utility Function

The best known utility function belonging to the directly additive class is the Klein-Rubin or Stone-Geary utility function,[15]

$$u(\boldsymbol{x}) = \sum_{i=1}^{k} \beta_i \log(x_i - \gamma_i) \qquad (2.40)$$

in which the β_i are constrained to be non-negative fractions summing to unity.

[15] L. R. Klein and H. Rubin, "A Constant Utility Index of the Cost of Living," *Review of Economic Studies* 15 (1948–49): 84–87; R. C. Geary, "A Note on 'A Constant Utility Index of the Cost of Living,'" *Review of Economic Studies* 18 (1950–51): 65–66.

The maximization of this utility function generates the linear expenditure system (LES) of Richard Stone, to be treated in Chapter 3.[16]

2.2.3 Frisch's Money Flexibility

From equation (2.28), recall the interpretation of ψ:

$$\psi = \frac{\lambda}{\partial\lambda/\partial m} \tag{2.28}$$

where λ is the marginal utility of (optimally allocated) total consumer spending. It is clear that ψ depends on the units in which m is measured. For ease of interpretation, ψ is best converted into an elasticity. The following elasticity

$$\omega = \frac{\partial\lambda}{\partial m}\frac{m}{\lambda} \tag{2.41}$$

namely, the elasticity of the marginal utility of spending with respect to spending, has been termed by Ragnar Frisch "the flexibility of the marginal utility of money" or, more simply, "money flexibility."[17] We note immediately the relation between ψ and ω:

$$\omega = m/\psi \tag{2.42}$$

In an oft-quoted passage Frisch has speculated on the welfare implications of ω and on its probable values.[18] Recently empirical estimates of ω have been collected by Sato who, however, totally rejects the cardinal features of Frisch's system.[19]

2.3 Barten's Almost Additive Preferences

The separability concepts discussed so far have been *exact* properties of the utility function. Barten's concept of *almost additive preferences*, on the other

---

[16] Richard Stone, "Linear Expenditure Systems and Demand Analysis: An Application to the Pattern of British Demand," *Economic Journal* 64, no. 255 (September 1954): 511–527.

[17] Ragnar Frisch, "A Complete Scheme for Computing All Direct and Cross Demand Elasticities in a Model with Many Sectors," *Econometrica* 27 (1959): 177–196.

[18] Ibid., p. 189.

[19] Kazuo Sato, "Additive Utility Functions with Double-Log Consumer Demand Functions," *Journal of Political Economy* 80, no. 1 (January–February 1972): 102–124.

hand, is defined in terms of an approximation involving the Hessian of the utility function. In a sense which will be made more precise below, the issue at stake is whether the Hessian $\boldsymbol{U}$ of the utility function is "sufficiently diagonal" to allow a certain convenient decomposition of its inverse to be made.

2.3.1 Almost Additive Preferences Defined

The definition of almost additive preferences devolves on the relative magnitudes of the on- and off-diagonal elements of $\boldsymbol{U}^{-1}$, the utility function's inverse Hessian. Let u_{ij} be the ijth element of the Hessian matrix $\boldsymbol{U}$. Then a *necessary* condition for almost additive preferences to pertain is that

$$\text{absf}\left(u_{ij}/\sqrt{u_{ii}u_{jj}}\right) < 1 \qquad \text{for all } i, j;\ i \neq j \tag{2.43}$$

[where absf( ) means absolute value of ( )]. If (2.43) is satisfied, a power-series expansion for $\boldsymbol{U}^{-1}$ is available. Let $\hat{\boldsymbol{U}}$ be $k \times k$ diagonal matrix whose iith element is $\sqrt{-u_{ii}}$ (zeros elsewhere).[20] That is, $\hat{\boldsymbol{U}}$ is defined by

$$-\hat{\boldsymbol{U}}\hat{\boldsymbol{U}} = \text{diag}(\boldsymbol{U}) \tag{2.44}$$

where diag( ) indicates the diagonal matrix whose elements are those appearing on the principal diagonal of ( ). Then it is clear that $\boldsymbol{U}$ can be written in the form

$$\boldsymbol{U} = -\hat{\boldsymbol{U}}(\boldsymbol{I}+\boldsymbol{H})\hat{\boldsymbol{U}} \tag{2.45}$$

where the matrix $\boldsymbol{H}$ is symmetric and has zeros on the principal diagonal. The off-diagonal elements h_{ij} of $\boldsymbol{H}$ are seen to satisfy

$$-h_{ij}\sqrt{u_{ii}u_{jj}} = u_{ij} \qquad (i \neq j) \tag{2.46}$$

If (2.43) holds true, then all of the h_{ij} are less than one in absolute value, and

---

[20] Well-behaved utility functions are assumed to have $u_{ii} \equiv \delta^2 u/(\delta x_i)^2 < 0$ for all i. This is an implication of the negative-definiteness of the bordered Hessian $\boldsymbol{V}$, defined in equations (1.25a & b).

This assumption of negative-definiteness is, in turn a *sufficient* condition to guarantee the existence of a constrained maximum of the utility function. It can, however, be shown that under *fairly* general conditions, negative-definiteness of $\boldsymbol{V}$ is both necessary and sufficient for the demand functions to be differentiable. See Phoebus J. Dhrymes, "On a Class of Utility and Production Functions Yielding Everywhere Differentiable Demand Functions," *Review of Economic Studies* 34, no. 4 (October 1967): 399–408.

the following expansion is available for $(\boldsymbol{I}+\boldsymbol{H})^{-1}$:[21]

$$(\boldsymbol{I}+\boldsymbol{H})^{-1} = \boldsymbol{I} - \boldsymbol{H} + \boldsymbol{H}^2 - \boldsymbol{H}^3 + \cdots \tag{2.47}$$

The idea of almost additive preferences is expressed by the following approximation, obtained by inverting (2.45) and dropping higher-order terms:

$$\begin{aligned} \boldsymbol{U}^{-1} &= -\hat{\boldsymbol{U}}^{-1}(\boldsymbol{I}-\boldsymbol{H}+\boldsymbol{H}^2-\boldsymbol{H}^3+\cdots)\hat{\boldsymbol{U}}^{-1} \\ &\doteq -\hat{\boldsymbol{U}}^{-1}(\boldsymbol{I}-\boldsymbol{H})\hat{\boldsymbol{U}}^{-1} \end{aligned} \tag{2.48}$$

If the approximation contained in the last line of (2.48) is, in a certain sense, "adequate," we shall say that almost additive preferences pertain.[22]

2.3.2 Substitution Effects Under Almost Additive Preferences

Substitution from the last line of (2.48) into (1.63) yields

$$\begin{aligned} \underset{k \times k}{[\kappa_{ij}]} &= -[\lambda\hat{\boldsymbol{U}}^{-1}(\boldsymbol{I}-\boldsymbol{H})\hat{\boldsymbol{U}}^{-1} + (\lambda/\lambda_m)\boldsymbol{x}_m\boldsymbol{x}_m^T] \\ &= -[\lambda\hat{\boldsymbol{U}}^{-1}(\boldsymbol{I}-\boldsymbol{H})\hat{\boldsymbol{U}}^{-1} + \psi\boldsymbol{x}_m\boldsymbol{x}_m^T] \end{aligned} \tag{2.49}$$

where ψ is λ/λ_m (which is consistent with (2.28)).

Equation (2.49) demonstrates that the specification of almost additive preferences does *not*, without further restrictions, accomplish any parsimony of parameterization. The elements of $\boldsymbol{H}$ are unknown—there are potentially $\frac{1}{2}k(k-1)$ distinct values—nothing has been gained beyond what was already available from the symmetry property of classical utility maximization. Further restrictions on $\boldsymbol{H}$ are therefore needed in operational applications. One possibility is to assume that all of the nondiagonal elements in $\boldsymbol{H}$ have the same value. The economic interpretation of this assumption is as follows: Consider any pair of commodities i and j $(i \neq j)$. The increase in the marginal utility of i resulting from a unit marginal increment in the consumption of j

---

[21] See George Hadley, *Linear Algebra* (Reading, Massachusetts: Addison-Wesley, 1965), pp. 116–119, for example.

[22] Strictly, one cannot define a concept by an approximation. When one states that "A approximately equals B," then *in vacuuo* the only logical content of this statement is that A does *not* equal B. For the statement to constitute a definition, precise values must be set on the limits of tolerable approximations. One approach to defining acceptable tolerance levels would be in terms of the observable implications (i.e., in terms of statistics derived on the basis of (2.48) from consumption data). For empirically orientated work, this seems to be a perfectly satisfactory way to proceed.

is proportional to the geometric average of the diminution in the marginal utility of i consequent upon a unit marginal increment in the consumption of i, and the diminution in the marginal utility of j caused by a unit marginal increment in the consumption of j. The constant of proportionality is independent of which pair $\{i, j\}$ of commodities is being considered. This is, admittedly, a somewhat elusive property of substitutability in the preference map and may not, therefore, appeal to many as a prior specification.[23]

2.3.3 Almost Additive, Block-Independent, Preferences

Almost additive preferences provide a simplification as compared with the general case; it does not lead directly, as we have seen, to any shrinkage of the parameter space. However, by specifying independence between certain pairs of commodities, the number of parameters may be reduced. This leads naturally to the specification of almost additive, block-independent preferences or "almost block additivity," which is the special case of block additivity (2.2) in which the preference functions $u^j(\mathbf{x}_j)$ defined on the different blocks $(j = 1, \ldots, n)$ each individually satisfy the definition of almost additivity. We take this up in an operational setting in Chapter 4, where the work of the Rotterdam School is discussed in more detail.

[23] At the date of writing, no empirical application along these lines was known to the author.

3 The Linear Expenditure System

3.1 Preliminary: The Transition from Utility Function to Behavioral Relations

In this section we devote some attention to a methodological point which must be understood before many econometric treatments of demand systems become intelligible. The solution of the basic maximum problem (1.15) generates a set of demand relations whose functional form depends on the form of the utility function. For some utility functions, the explicit functional form of the demand functions has been derived in the literature;[1] in the great majority of cases, though, explicit functional forms for demand equations either do not exist or else remain to be derived. In many cases in which they have been derived these demand relations turn out to be highly nonlinear in their parameters;[2] they are not readily amenable, therefore, to econometric estimation.

In the circumstances, many econometricians have preferred to work with an arbitrary (but manageable) functional form imposed on the behavioral relations estimated (i.e., on demand functions or expenditure relations, usually). This would be a self-defeating approach if thereby all of the information inherent in the structure of the maximum problem were lost. The way to avoid this is to enforce restrictions coming from the structure of the problem at some *local* set of coordinates (often sample means). It is, of course, true that the theoretically correct functional form of the behavioral relations would satisfy these restrictions *globally*, but the disadvantages of attempting to fit the

---

[1] For the Stone-Geary utility function, see, e.g., Richard Stone, "Linear Expenditure Systems and Demand Analysis: An Application to the Pattern of British Demand," *Economic Journal* 64, no. 255 (September 1954): 511–527; for the indirect addilog system see H. S. Houthakker, "Additive Preferences," *Econometrica* 28, no. 2 (April 1960): 244–257; for certain cases of the Johansen generalization of Stone-Geary, see Leif Johansen, "On the Relationships Between Some Systems of Demand Functions," University of Oslo, Institute of Economics, *Reprint Series No. 47*, Oslo, 1969; reprinted from *Liiketaloudellinen Aikakauskirja*. (See also footnote 2.)

[2] See e.g., the results obtained for the *s*-Branch utility tree by Murray Brown and Dale Heien, "The *S*-Branch Utility Tree: A Generalization of the Linear Expenditure System," *Econometrica* 40, no. 4 (July 1972): 737–747. The theoretical development contributed by Brown and Heien is summarized in Chapter 5.

exact system often outweigh this advantage. In many samples, moreover, the range of variation of the variables is such that the restrictions are satisfied to a good approximation at all data points.

In some rare cases the nonlinearities of the exact set of behavioral relations are moderate and estimation is not too difficult—in this connection we discuss below the work of Stone, Parks, and Solari on the linear expenditure system. In a few cases where the nonlinearities are formidable some talented workers backed by first-class computing laboratories and large computing budgets have been able to estimate the demand functions in their exact form.[3] But the majority of econometric work has been based on the method of *local enforcement of demand-theoretic restrictions.*[4]

One further point needs elaboration. In enforcing restrictions among demand relations, one does not necessarily assume a specific functional form. In Chapter 1 we have seen that a very wide class of functional forms would generate demand functions subject to additivity, symmetry, and homogeneity. Similarly, in Chapter 2, constraints among derivatives—see (2.39) for example—are derived for utility functions belonging to certain classes. The bulk of the empirical work[5] remains agnostic about particular functional forms of the utility functions, being based rather on the assumption that the utility function belongs to some particular class (such as the directly additive class).

3.2 Principal Features of Stone's System

3.2.1 Expenditure System Defined

Using a notation similar to that of Chapter 1, let the demand function for good i be

$$x_{it} = D_i(\boldsymbol{p}_t; m_t) \qquad (i = 1, \ldots, k) \tag{3.1}$$

[3] The most widely estimated "exact" system (in this sense) is the linear expenditure system—references will be found below. Perhaps the most complicated system whose demand functions have been fitted in exact form is the s-branch utility function—see Brown and Heien, op. cit.

[4] The Rotterdam School work follows the local enforcement rule, as in, e.g., Anton Barten, "Maximum Likelihood Estimation of a Complete System of Demand Equations," *European Economic Review* 1, no. 1 (Fall 1969): 7–73; Henri Theil, "The Information Approach to Demand Analysis," *Econometrica* 33, no. 1 (January 1965): 67–87. The same approach is taken by many other authors. See, e.g., Ray Byron, "Methods for Estimating Demand Equations Using Prior Information: A Series of Experiments with Australian Data," *Australian Economic Papers* 7, no. 11 (December 1968): 227–248; Alan Powell, "A Complete System of Consumer Demand Equations for the Australian Economy Fitted by a Model of Additive Preferences," *Econometrica* 34, no. 3 (July 1966): 661–675.

[5] Including the references cited in footnote 4.

in which $\boldsymbol{p}_t$ is the vector of all k prices, and m_t is total expenditure ("income"). As before, the subscript t is for dating. Multiply both sides of (3.1) by i's price:

$$p_{it}x_{it} \equiv v_{it} = p_{it}D_i(\boldsymbol{p}_t; m_t) \qquad (i = 1, \ldots, k) \tag{3.2}$$

We refer to (3.2) as an *expenditure system.* In the case in which the RHS of (3.2) turns out to be linear in all prices and in income, we have a *linear expenditure system.* Such a system can be written

$$v_{it} = c_i + \sum_{j=1}^{k} a_{ij}\, p_{jt} + \beta_i m_t \tag{3.3}$$

3.2.2 Review of Major Results

Stone's linear expenditure system (LES) is exhaustively treated in a justly famous monograph by Arthur Goldberger.[6] The principal results are briefly recapitulated below.

i. The only linear expenditure system globally compatible with the maximization of a classical utility function is *the* linear expenditure system in which

$$a_{ij} = -\beta_i\gamma_j \qquad (\text{for } i \neq j) \tag{3.4a}$$

and

$$a_{ii} = \gamma_i(1-\beta_i) \qquad (\text{for } i = j) \tag{3.4b}$$

for some constants γ_i $(i = 1, \ldots, k)$; and in which

$$c_i \equiv 0 \qquad (\text{all } i) \tag{3.4c}$$

as well as

$$\sum_{j=1}^{k} \beta_j \equiv 1 \qquad 0 < \beta_i < 1 \quad (\text{all } i) \tag{3.4d}$$

Thus *the* LES may be written

$$v_{it} = p_{it}\gamma_i + \beta_i\left(m_t - \sum_{j=1}^{k} p_{jt}\gamma_j\right) \tag{3.5}$$

---

[6] Arthur S. Goldberger, "Functional Form and Utility: A Review of Consumer Demand Theory," University of Wisconsin, Social Systems Research Institute, Systems Formulation, Methodology and Policy Workshop Paper 6703, October 1967.

ii. There is one and only one utility function whose maximization leads to the LES; namely, the Stone-Geary (or Klein-Rubin) utility function

$$u(x_t) = \sum_{i=1}^{k} \beta_i \log(x_{it} - \gamma_i) \tag{3.6}$$

This function is directly additive.

iii. In the LES there cannot exist complements or inferior goods. This can be seen as follows.[7] The nonsatiety axiom of demand theory requires that

$$\partial u/\partial x_{it} > 0 \tag{3.7}$$

i.e., that

$$\beta_i (x_{it} - \gamma_i)^{-1} > 0 \tag{3.8}$$

But the utility function is only defined for $x_{it} > \gamma_i$. Hence $(x_{it} - \gamma_i)^{-1}$ is positive, and (3.8) then requires that $\beta_i > 0$, ruling out inferior goods. The Slutsky substitution term—the compensated cross-price derivative of consumption of good i with respect to the price of j as defined in (1.38) and (1.63)—within the LES takes the following form:

$$\kappa_{ij}(t) = \frac{\beta_i (x_{jt} - \gamma_j)}{p_i} \tag{3.9}$$

Since, for data points t at which the utility index u is defined, the expression $(x_{jt} - \gamma_j)$ is positive, as are prices and marginal budget shares $\boldsymbol{\beta}$, the substitution term is unambiguously positive. Hence all pairs $\{i, j\}$ are *substitutes* in the LES.

iv. All price elasticities of demand in the LES are less than unity in absolute value unless some of the parameters γ_i are permitted to be negative The own-price elasticity of the ith commodity is

$$\eta_{ii}(t) = \frac{(1 - \beta_i)\gamma_i}{x_{it}} - 1 \tag{3.10}$$

We have seen that $0 < \beta_i < 1$ (all i), and that $0 < x_{it} > \gamma_i$ whenever the utility function is defined. The only way in which $\eta_{ii}(t)$ can become less than -1 (i.e., greater than 1 in absolute value) is for its γ_i value to be negative.

---

[7] The material on this point draws on the exposition of Howe. See Howard Howe, "Preliminary Estimates of the Linear and Quadratic Expenditure Systems," University of Pennsylvania, Department of Economics, mimeo (December 14, 1972), p. 80.

v. The LES may be *nested.* Let

$$u(\boldsymbol{x}) = u(x_1, \ldots, x_k)$$

and let some subsets of the x's be aggregated into a new set of categories with identifying indexes s, $s = 1, \ldots, S$. Let expenditure on the x's contained within s be $v_{.st}$. Then, by construction,

$$v_{.st} = \sum_{i \in s} v_{it} \tag{3.11}$$

Let

$$\beta_{.s} = \sum_{i \in s} \beta_i \tag{3.12}$$

Then the LES (3.5) may be written,[8]

$$v_{.st} = p_{.st}\gamma_{.s} + \beta_{.s}\left(m_t - \sum_{s=1}^{S} p_{.st}\gamma_{.s}\right) \qquad (s = 1, \ldots, S) \tag{3.13a}$$

$$v_{jt} = p_{jt}\gamma_j + \frac{\beta_j}{\beta_{.s}}\left(v_{.st} - \sum_{j \in s} p_{jt}\gamma_j\right) \qquad (j \in s;\ s = 1, \ldots, S) \tag{3.13b}$$

in which

$$\gamma_{.s} = \sum_{j \in s} \gamma_j \tag{3.13c}$$

and

$$p_{.st} = \sum_{j \in s} \frac{\gamma_j}{\sum_{j \in s} \gamma_j} p_{jt} \tag{3.13d}$$

Note that it is the expenditure system that nests, *not* the utility function (which remains directly additive). For an example, suppose that all consumption expenditure has been classified into the following *seven* categories:

Food	Entertainment
Clothing	Public Transportation
Housing	Private Transportation
	Other

Then the nesting property implies that if the utility function is directly additive in these items, one could write the corresponding LES either as involving the

[8] See Richard Stone, *Mathematical Models of the Economy and Other Essays* (London: Chapman and Hall, 1970), pp. 85–86.

seven commodities listed above, or aggregates thereof. In particular, the LES could be written as involving the *six* categories obtained when the two transportation categories are merged. The subsidiary allocation equation corresponding to (3.13b) in this example would be a linear expenditure subsystem in which the left-hand variables are expenditures on public and private transportation, and in which the right-hand "income" variable $v_{.st}$ is total transportation expenditure. The only two price variables appearing explicitly in this subsystem are the prices of public and private transportation. Ignoring for the present problems created by the endogeneity of the right-hand variables $v_{.st}$ in the subsystem (3.13b), one could follow Stone's suggestion and estimate the system as follows:

> *Step 1.* Obtain estimates of $\gamma_{.s}$ and $\beta_{.s}$ working with the larger aggregates, and using whatever price indicators are available as estimates of the $p_{.st}$.
>
> *Step 2.* Estimate the γ_j and $(\beta_j/\beta_{.s})$ from the subsystem, recovering individual marginal budget shares for the aggregands by multiplying estimated $(\beta_j/\beta_{.s})$ values by $\beta_{.s}$ estimates from Step 1.

Stone does not consider the internal consistency of the price aggregation procedure. It is clear that to ensure consistency the γ_j's obtained from Step 2 would have to be constrained to sum to the appropriate $\gamma_{.s}$'s in line with (3.13c).

vi. The Frisch parameter within the LES is the inverse of the negative of the "supernumerary ratio." If by "supernumerary income" we mean

$$z_t = \left(m_t - \sum_{j=1}^{k} p_{jt}\gamma_j\right) \tag{3.14}$$

then the supernumerary ratio is

$$r_t = \frac{z_t}{m_t} \tag{3.15}$$

with negative inverse

$$\frac{-1}{r_t} = \frac{-m_t}{z_t} \tag{3.16}$$

Goldberger shows that this expression may be identified with the Frisch parameter ω of (2.42).

vii. The various elasticity formulae pertinent to the LES are listed in Table 3–1.

Table 3–1

Elasticity Formulae for the Linear Expenditure System

Description	Own[a]	Cross[b]
Ordinary price elasticity	$\eta_{ii}(t) = [(1-\beta_i)\gamma_i/x_{it}] - 1$	$\eta_{ij}(t) = -\beta_i\gamma_j p_{jt}/v_{it}$
Compensated price elasticity	$\varepsilon_{ii}(t) = -(1-\beta_i)(1-\gamma_i/x_{it})$	$\varepsilon_{ij}(t) = \beta_j(1-\gamma_i/x_{it})$
Elasticity of substitution[c]	$\sigma_{ii}(t) = m_t\varepsilon_{ii}(t)/v_{it}$	$\sigma_{ij}(t) = m_t\varepsilon_{ij}(t)/v_{jt}$
Total expenditure elasticity	$E_i(t) = \beta_i m_t/v_t$	
Frisch "parameter": Elasticity of the marginal utility of total expenditure with respect to total expenditure	$\omega(t) = -m_t/(m_t - p_t^T\gamma)$	

[a] Elasticity of consumption of good i with respect to price of i.
[b] Elasticity of consumption of good i with respect to price of j ($j \neq i$).
[c] Assumes perfect competition in consumer goods market.

viii. Income effects swamp substitution effects so that all goods are *gross* complements in the LES; i.e., although compensated cross elasticities ε_{ij} are positive (*net* substitutability), uncompensated cross price elasticities η_{ij} are negative (for all pairs $\{i, j\}$ with $i \neq j$).

3.3 Estimation of Stone's System

3.3.1 Systems Least-Squares Approach (*Stone*)

Stone's early estimations of the LES were carried out without appeal to any explicit principle of statistical inference.[9] Rather, the basis of estimation was the descriptive statistical criterion of best fit. The "best fit" sought was the set of parameters $\{\beta_1, \ldots, \beta_k; \gamma_1, \ldots, \gamma_k\}$ giving the minimum unweighted sum of squares for the overall system; i.e., the minimand selected was

$$SST = \sum_{j=1}^{k} \sum_{t=1}^{N} [v_{jt} - p_{jt}\gamma_j - \beta_j(m_t - p_t^T\gamma)]^2 \qquad (3.17)$$

in which γ is the k-order column vector with typical element γ_i, and N is the number of data points. The cross product involving β's and γ's in the above expression is the critical nonlinearity in determining the vectors $\hat{\boldsymbol{\beta}}$ and $\hat{\gamma}$ which yield the minimum of SST. However, for fixed $\boldsymbol{\beta}$ or fixed γ, the basic LES equation is linear in the other parameter vector. If we write u_{it} as the residual

[9] Stone, "Linear Expenditure Systems . . .," op. cit.

from the tth data point of the ith commodity equation, we have alternatively either

$$u_{it} = (v_{it} - \gamma_i p_{it}) - \beta_i(m_t - \boldsymbol{p}_t^T \boldsymbol{\gamma}) \tag{3.18}$$

$$= w_{it} - \beta_i z_t \qquad \text{(say)} \tag{3.19}$$

when $\boldsymbol{\gamma}$ is fixed; or when $\boldsymbol{\beta}$ is fixed,

$$u_{it} = (v_{it} - \beta_i m_t) - [-\beta_i p_{1t}, -\beta_i p_{2t}, \ldots, -\beta_i p_{i-1,t}$$

$$+ (1-\beta_i)p_{it}, -\beta_i p_{i+1,t}, \ldots, -\beta_i p_{kt}]^T \boldsymbol{\gamma} \tag{3.20}$$

$$= W_{it} - \underset{1\times k}{\boldsymbol{Z}_{it}^T} \underset{k\times 1}{\boldsymbol{\gamma}} \qquad \text{(say)} \tag{3.21}$$

Note that with $\boldsymbol{\gamma}$ fixed the set of k LES equations of (3.5) are a set of k homogeneous regression equations involving the *same* regressor, z_t. Two properties follow immediately:

First. A systems Aitken approach to the estimation of (3.19) would yield identically the same results as ordinary least squares (OLS) applied *seriatim* to each commodity equation.[10] That is, a weighted sum of squares with *any* finite weights is minimized by applying the simple OLS technique. In particular, the weighted sum of squares in which all weights are unity is minimized. Hence for given $\boldsymbol{\gamma}$, SST is minimized by applying OLS to each of the k equations (3.19).

Second. Since the w_{it} sum over i to z_t, the β_i estimated by applying OLS *seriatim* to equations (3.19) satisfy the requirement

$$\hat{\boldsymbol{\beta}}^T \mathbf{1} = 1 \tag{3.22}$$

in which $\hat{\boldsymbol{\beta}}$ is the value of $\boldsymbol{\beta}$ obtained by selecting the OLSE's $\hat{\beta}_1, \ldots, \hat{\beta}_k$; and $\mathbf{1}$ is a column vector of k units.[11]

Now consider the representation of the system with $\boldsymbol{\beta}$ fixed. In the set of equations (3.21), it is the regressors $\boldsymbol{Z}_{it}$ that vary among equations ($i = 1, \ldots, k$);

---

[10] Arnold Zellner, "An Efficient Method of Estimating Seemingly Unrelated Regressions and Tests for Aggregation Bias," *Journal of the American Statistical Association* 57, no. 298 (June 1962): 348–368.

[11] See, e.g., Alan Powell, "Aitken Estimators as a Tool in Allocating Predetermined Aggregates," *Journal of the American Statistical Association* 64, no. 327 (September 1969): 913–922.

the regression coefficient vector γ, on the other hand, is the same in all equations.

To find the values of the γ's which minimize SST, equations (3.21) must be treated as a system. The minimand becomes

$$SS_\beta = \sum_{i=1}^{k} \sum_{t=1}^{N} (W_{it} - Z_{it}^T \gamma)^2 \tag{3.23}$$

The first-order condition for a minimum is

$$\sum_i \sum_t W_{it} \boldsymbol{Z}_{it} = \left(\sum_i \sum_t \underset{k \times 1}{\boldsymbol{Z}_{it}} \underset{1 \times k}{\boldsymbol{Z}_{it}^T} \right) \gamma \tag{3.24}$$

that is, the required estimate is

$$\hat{\gamma} = \left(\sum_i \sum_t \boldsymbol{Z}_{it} \boldsymbol{Z}_{it}^T \right)^{-1} \sum_i \sum_t W_{it} \boldsymbol{Z}_{it} \tag{3.25}$$

Stone's procedure for finding the minimum of SST was to pass iteratively between the OLSE of $\boldsymbol{\beta}$—which has the typical element

$$\hat{\beta}_i = \sum_{t=1}^{N} w_{it} z_t \div \sum_{t=1}^{N} z_t^2 \tag{3.26}$$

—and the estimate (3.25) of γ. At convergence, the computed $\hat{\boldsymbol{\beta}}$ and $\hat{\gamma}$ do not change with further iterations, and a minimum of SST is located. However, because no inferential equipment is used in the procedure, nothing can be said about the standard errors of the estimates obtained.

3.3.2 *Systems Least-Squares Approach* (*Carlevaro and Rossier*)

Whilst the documented empirical record suggests that Stone's search procedure has had a good record for convergence, the convergence is typically slow. Two members of Solari's Econometric Laboratory at the University of Geneva, Carlevaro and Rossier, have programmed a more efficient method of locating the minimum of SST.[12] This is a linearization procedure with general applicability for locating the least-squares solution for a nonlinear function

[12] F. Carlevaro and E. Rossier, "Le Programme Linex pour l'Estimation des Parametres du Systeme Lineaire de Depenses," Faculté des Sciences Économiques et Sociales, Université de Genève, Centre d'Econometrie, Cahier 15/6/70 June 1970 pp. 21–23.

of an unknown set of parameters.[13] Suppose that in

$$y_t \doteq f_t(\mathbf{\Theta}) \qquad (t = 1, \ldots, n) \tag{3.27}$$

the f_t's are a set of functions of an unknown k vector, $\mathbf{\Theta}$; it is desired to find that value of $\mathbf{\Theta}$ (namely, $\hat{\mathbf{\Theta}}$) which minimizes

$$S = \sum_{t=1}^{N} [y_t - f_t(\mathbf{\Theta})]^2 \tag{3.28}$$

Further, let f_t be a set of functions for which the following representation is valid:

$$f_t(\mathbf{\Theta}) = \xi_{t\Theta}^T \mathbf{\Theta} \qquad (t = 1, \ldots, N) \tag{3.29}$$

in which $\xi_{t\Theta}$ is a k vector which depends on data observed at t, as well as depending on the value of $\mathbf{\Theta}$. Collecting all N functions f_t we could write

$$\underset{N \times 1}{\mathbf{f}(\mathbf{\Theta})} = \underset{N \times k}{\xi_\Theta} \; \underset{k \times 1}{\mathbf{\Theta}} \tag{3.30}$$

as a matrix representation of (3.29). Let $\mathbf{\Theta}^\circ$ be some initial guess at $\mathbf{\Theta}$; let the corresponding value of ξ_Θ be ξ_Θ°. Then

$$\mathbf{f}(\mathbf{\Theta}) = (\xi_\Theta - \xi_\Theta^\circ)(\mathbf{\Theta} - \mathbf{\Theta}^\circ) + \xi_\Theta^\circ(\mathbf{\Theta} - \mathbf{\Theta}^\circ) + \xi_\Theta \mathbf{\Theta}^\circ \tag{3.31}$$

Writing

$$\Delta\mathbf{\Theta} = \mathbf{\Theta} - \mathbf{\Theta}^\circ \tag{3.32a}$$

and

$$\Delta\xi_\Theta = \xi_\Theta - \xi_\Theta^\circ \tag{3.32b}$$

(3.31) becomes

$$\mathbf{f}(\mathbf{\Theta}) = \Delta\xi_\Theta \, \Delta\mathbf{\Theta} + \xi_\Theta^\circ \, \Delta\mathbf{\Theta} + \xi_\Theta \mathbf{\Theta}^\circ \tag{3.33}$$

Neglecting the first term on the right of (3.33) and using the approximation

$$\xi_\Theta^\circ \mathbf{\Theta}^\circ \doteq \xi_\Theta \mathbf{\Theta}^\circ \tag{3.34}$$

---

[13] D. W. Marquardt, "An Algorithm for Least Squares Estimation of Non-Linear Parameters," *Journal of the Society of Industrial and Applied Mathematics* 11, no. 2 (1963): 431–441.

we obtain, as an approximation to (3.31),

$$\boldsymbol{f}(\boldsymbol{\Theta}) \doteq \xi_{\Theta}^{\circ}\,\boldsymbol{\Theta}^{\circ} + \xi_{\Theta}^{\circ}\,\Delta\boldsymbol{\Theta} \tag{3.35a}$$

that is

$$(\boldsymbol{f}(\boldsymbol{\Theta}) - \xi_{\Theta}^{\circ}\,\boldsymbol{\Theta}^{\circ}) \doteq \xi_{\Theta}^{\circ}\,\Delta\boldsymbol{\Theta} \tag{3.35b}$$

In an econometric setting the functions f_t will be approximately equal to some set of realized values of a left-hand variable of interest. Typically, we would specify

$$y_t = f_t(\boldsymbol{\Theta}) + (\text{zero mean random error}) \tag{3.36}$$

in which case, $f_t(\boldsymbol{\Theta})$ in (3.27) is just the expected value of y_t. The vector $\boldsymbol{y}$ of realizations on y_t can be used to approximate $\boldsymbol{f}(\boldsymbol{\Theta})$ in (3.35b). It follows that, given an initial value of $\boldsymbol{\Theta}$, the OLSE of $\Delta\boldsymbol{\Theta}$ in (3.35b), namely,

$$\widehat{\Delta\boldsymbol{\Theta}} = [(\xi_{\Theta}^{\circ})^T \xi_{\Theta}^{\circ}]^{-1} (\xi_{\Theta}^{\circ})^T (\boldsymbol{y} - \xi_{\Theta}^{\circ}\,\boldsymbol{\Theta}^{\circ}) \tag{3.37}$$

is computable. This estimated increment may be added to $\boldsymbol{\Theta}^{\circ}$ in order to obtain new estimates of $\boldsymbol{\Theta}$ and of ξ_{Θ}°, and the whole procedure iterated. It can be proved that if this procedure converges so that $\widehat{\Delta\boldsymbol{\Theta}} = \boldsymbol{0}$, it converges to a minimum of (3.28).

In the context of the LES we write the expenditure system as a whole, as

$$\begin{bmatrix} \boldsymbol{v}_1 \\ \boldsymbol{v}_2 \\ \vdots \\ \boldsymbol{v}_k \end{bmatrix} = \left[\begin{array}{cccc:cccc} \boldsymbol{p}^1 & \boldsymbol{0} & \cdots & \boldsymbol{0} & (\boldsymbol{m}-\boldsymbol{P}\gamma) & \boldsymbol{0} & \cdots & \boldsymbol{0} \\ \boldsymbol{0} & \boldsymbol{p}^2 & & \boldsymbol{0} & \boldsymbol{0} & (\boldsymbol{m}-\boldsymbol{P}\gamma) & \cdots & \boldsymbol{0} \\ \vdots & \vdots & & \vdots & \vdots & \vdots & & \\ \boldsymbol{0} & \boldsymbol{0} & \cdots & \boldsymbol{p}^k & \boldsymbol{0} & \boldsymbol{0} & \cdots & (\boldsymbol{m}-\boldsymbol{P}\gamma) \end{array}\right] \begin{bmatrix} \gamma \\ \hdashline \boldsymbol{\beta} \end{bmatrix}$$

$$+ \ (\text{random error}) \tag{3.38a}$$

in which $\boldsymbol{v}_i$ is the N-order column vector of observations on v_{it}; $\boldsymbol{m}$ is the observation vector on m_t, and has similar dimension; $\boldsymbol{P}$ is the $N \times k$ matrix of observations on the k prices; and $\boldsymbol{p}^j$ is the jth column of $\boldsymbol{P}$. A more compact notation for (3.38a) is

$$\boldsymbol{v} = \boldsymbol{Z\alpha} + (\text{random error}) \tag{3.38b}$$

In terms of the proceeding discussion, we identify $\boldsymbol{v}$ with $\boldsymbol{y}$, $\boldsymbol{Z}$ with ξ_{Θ}, and $\boldsymbol{\alpha}$

Table 3–2

Stone's Linear Expenditure System Fitted to Australian National Accounts Data, 1948–1949 through 1966–1967: Principal Results of Systems Least-Squares Fit

Commodity Group	Estimates of					
	Marginal Budget Share	Total Expenditure Elasticity[a]	Stone-Geary Parameter[b]	Own Price Elasticity[a]	Quasi-R^2	Durbin-Watson Statistic
i	β_i	E_i	γ_i	η_{ii}	[c]	
1. Food	.1057	.428	217.29	−.195	.9961	.891
2. Tobacco & drink	.0628	.607	91.07	−.135	.9904	.617
3. Clothing	.0440	.353	99.77	−.079	.9179	.742
4. Household durables	.1139	1.424	45.32	−.317	.9764	.855
5. Housing & fuel	.2569	2.219	74.49	−.494	.9916	1.148
6. Public transportation	0	0	39.99	0	.9252	0.263
7. Private transportation	.2091	2.544	38.34	−.566	.9506	1.441
8. Services	.1988	1.488	94.36	−.331	.9977	1.635
9. Other	.0089	.119	82.07	−.026	.9661	1.472
Sum	1.000		782.70[d]			

[a] Evaluated at sample mean values of average budget shares.
[b] Units are Australian dollars at prices of 1966–1967 (per capita).
[c] $1 - \left(\sum_{t=1}^{N} \hat{u}_{it}^{2'} \div \sum_{t=1}^{N} v_{it}^2 \right).$
[d] Units are Australian dollars of 1966–1967 purchasing power (per capita).

with $\mathbf{\Theta}$. Experience with the linearization algorithm as coded by Carlevaro and Rossier indicates that the method is both robust and computationally efficient.[14]

Some Australian results obtained by this method are given in Table 3–2. The data were basically national accounts statistics on a per capita basis, with implicit deflators used as price indicators wherever possible. The computer program LINEX[15] was used to obtain a systems least squares fit. This program searches for $\boldsymbol{\beta}$ only over non-negative values. Six-digit convergence was achieved in 29 iterations. In the case of Public Transportation this resulted in a corner solution; i.e., a $\hat{\beta}_i$ value of zero. The solution value of $\boldsymbol{\beta}$ is to be interpreted, therefore, as locating a constrained minimum of SST. The result is not implausible since over the relevant data period Public Transportation has contained one component that is probably an inferior good (namely, train, tram, and bus travel) and another that is a normal good (air travel). The exceptionally high estimated income elasticity for Housing is probably associated with the postwar elimination of demand back-logs and gradual dismantling of wartime controls. The Durbin-Watson statistics suggest that serial correlation is a problem. It is not clear whether the difficulty lies in the linearity of the Engel curves within LES, or whether a more subtle misspecification is involved.

3.3.3 Maximum-Likelihood Approach (Parks and Solari)

The estimation of the LES was put on a firmer statistical footing by the independent, concurrent, work of Parks and Solari.[16] As in the case of Stone's procedure, the key to their successful treatment of the problem was their ability to write down partially linear representations of the system of the type shown by (3.19) and (3.21). An initial complication, however, arises from the

[14] Using Carlevaro and Rossier's program LINEX (as documented in Carlevaro and Rossier, op. cit.) on national accounts data for 8 commodities in 21 countries Lluch and Powell ("International Comparisons of Expenditure and Saving Patterns," Development Research Center, World Bank, January 1973) encountered only two cases in which the method failed to converge.

[15] Carlevaro and Rossier, op. cit.

[16] Richard Parks, "Systems of Demand Equations: An Empirical Comparison of Alternative Functional Forms," *Econometrica* 37, no. 4 (October 1969): 629–650; "Maximum Likelihood Estimation of the Linear Expenditure System," *Journal of the American Statistical Association* 66, no. 336 (December 1971): pp. 900–903. Luigi Solari, "Sur L'estimation du Systeme Lineaire de Depenses Par La Methode du Maximum de Vraisemblance," Centre D'Econometrie, Cahier FN/5243.1/3, Faculté des Sciences Économiques et Sociales, Universite de Genève, Mars 1969 (mimeo, p. 40); *Theori des Choix et Fonctions de Consommation Semi-Agregées, Modeles Statistiques* (Geneva: Dros, 1971).

impact of the budget constraint

$$\sum_i v_{it} \equiv m_t$$

on the error term. If a zero-mean random error e_{it} is added to the RHS of (3.5), it follows that

$$\sum_{i=1}^{k} e_{it} \equiv 0 \tag{3.39}$$

The contemporaneous covariance matrix of the e_{it}'s, therefore, is singular. That is

$$\begin{aligned} |\boldsymbol{\Omega}| &= \begin{vmatrix} \omega_{11} & \omega_{12} & \cdots & \omega_{1k} \\ \vdots & & & \vdots \\ \omega_{k1} & & \cdots & \omega_{kk} \end{vmatrix} \\ &= \begin{vmatrix} Ee_{1t}^2 & \cdots & Ee_{1t}e_{kt} \\ \vdots & & \vdots \\ Ee_{kt}e_{1t} & \cdots & Ee_{kt}^2 \end{vmatrix} \\ &= 0 \end{aligned} \tag{3.40}$$

Since the inverse of the covariance matrix appears in the likelihood function, this presents an apparent difficulty for the application of the maximum-likelihood principle. However, several authors have demonstrated that the appropriate solution to this problem is to drop one of the equations of the system. The resultant subsystem of $(k-1)$ commodity equations has a contemporaneous covariance matrix of full rank. It has been shown that the maximum-likelihood estimators (and indeed any estimators of the Aitken family) are invariant under the choice of which equation is deleted.[17]

Parks and Solari both assume that the error terms e_{it} are joint normally distributed with stationary variances and (contemporaneous) covariances, ω_{ij}, but that all own- and cross-lag covariances vanish; i.e., that

$$E(e_{it}e_{j\tau}) = 0 \qquad \text{(whenever } t \neq \tau) \tag{3.41}$$

so that the covariance properties of the system are fully characterized by the

---

[17] Barten, "Maximum Likelihood Estimation . . .," op. cit.; Parks, "Maximum Likelihood Estimation . . .," op. cit.; Solari, "Sur L'Estimation du Systeme Lineaire . . .," op. cit.; Arshad Zaman, "Formulation and Estimation of a Complete System of Demand Equations," Department of Economics, Michigan State University, *Econometrics Workshop Special Report No. 3*, September 1970, pp. vi, 227; Powell, "Aitken Estimators . . .," op. cit.

matrix $\boldsymbol{\Omega}$. To facilitate manipulation of the likelihood function, the expressions (3.19) and (3.21) can be written in matrix form. Equation (3.19) becomes,[18]

$$\underset{kN\times 1}{\begin{bmatrix} w_1 \\ w_2 \\ \vdots \\ w_k \end{bmatrix}} = \underset{kN\times k}{\begin{bmatrix} z & 0 & \cdots & 0 \\ 0 & z & \cdots & 0 \\ \vdots & & & \\ 0 & 0 & \cdots & z \end{bmatrix}} \underset{k\times 1}{\boldsymbol{\beta}} + \underset{kN\times 1}{\begin{bmatrix} e_1 \\ e_2 \\ \vdots \\ e_k \end{bmatrix}} \tag{3.42a}$$

Deleting the last equation in order to obtain a system with covariance matrix of full rank, and compacting the notation, we have[19]

$$\underset{(k-1)N\times 1}{w} = \underset{(k-1)N\times(k-1)}{z^*} \underset{(k-1)\times 1}{\boldsymbol{\beta}^{\circ}} + \underset{(k-1)N\times 1}{e} \tag{3.42b}$$

In (3.42b), the matrix z^* is

$$z^* = I_{(k-1)} \otimes z \tag{3.42c}$$

in which $\otimes$ is the Kronecker product operation. Equation (3.21) becomes

$$\underset{kN\times 1}{\begin{bmatrix} W_1 \\ W_2 \\ \vdots \\ W_k \end{bmatrix}} = \underset{kN\times k}{\begin{bmatrix} Z_1 \\ Z_2 \\ \vdots \\ Z_k \end{bmatrix}} \underset{k\times 1}{\gamma} + \underset{kN\times 1}{\begin{bmatrix} e_1 \\ e_2 \\ \vdots \\ e_k \end{bmatrix}} \tag{3.43a}$$

in which W_i is the N-order column vector with typical element W_{it}, and Z_i is the $N \times k$ matrix whose tth row is Z_{it}^T. After deletion of the kth equation, a more compact notation for (3.43a) is

$$\underset{(k-1)N\times 1}{W} = \underset{(k-1)N\times k}{Z^*} \underset{k\times 1}{\gamma} + \underset{(k-1)N\times 1}{e} \tag{3.43b}$$

If the contemporaneous covariance matrix of the truncated system (obtained by deletion of the last row and column of $\boldsymbol{\Omega}$) is $\boldsymbol{\Omega}^*$, then the (log) likelihood

[18] Parks, "Maximum Likelihood Estimation of the Linear Expenditure System," op. cit., p. 900.

[19] Where $\boldsymbol{\beta}^{\circ}$ is the $(k-1)$ order subvector of $\boldsymbol{\beta}$ obtained by deleting its last element.

function of the system is

$$L \equiv L(e \mid \beta, \gamma, \Omega) \tag{3.44a}$$

$$\equiv -(k-1)\frac{N}{2}\log(2\pi) - \frac{N}{2}\log|\Omega^*| - \tfrac{1}{2}e^T[(\Omega^*)^{-1} \otimes I_N]e$$

In view of (3.42b) and (3.43b), the log likelihood function may be written either as

$$L(e \mid \beta, \gamma, \Omega) = \text{constant} - \frac{N}{2}\log|\Omega^*|$$

$$-\tfrac{1}{2}\{(w - z^*\beta^\circ)^T[(\Omega^*)^{-1} \otimes I_N](w - z^*\beta^\circ)\} \tag{3.44b}$$

or as

$$L(e \mid \beta, \gamma, \Omega) = \text{constant} - \frac{N}{2}\log|\Omega^*|$$

$$-\tfrac{1}{2}\{(W - Z^*\gamma)^T[(\Omega^*)^{-1} \otimes I_N](W - Z^*\gamma)\} \tag{3.44c}$$

It follows that the first-order conditions for a maximum of L have a particularly simple matrix representation. Differentiating L in its representation (3.44b) with respect to β° and in its representation (3.44c) with respect to γ, these first-order conditions yield the estimators,

$$\hat{\beta}^\circ = \{(z^*)^T[(\Omega^*)^{-1} \otimes I_N]z^*\}^{-1}(z^*)^T[(\Omega^*)^{-1} \otimes I_N]w \tag{3.45a}$$

and

$$\hat{\gamma} = \{(Z^*)^T[(\Omega^*)^{-1} \otimes I_N]Z^*\}^{-1}(Z^*)^T[(\Omega^*)^{-1} \otimes I_N]W \tag{3.45b}$$

Each of these will be recognized as an Aitken estimator based on a partial linearization of the system, and on Ω^*. To make the procedure operational an estimator of Ω^* is required for insertion into (3.45a, and b). Differentiation of L with respect to the elements of Ω^* yields, after some manipulation, the following (common sense) estimator:

$$\hat{\Omega}^* = \frac{1}{N}\begin{bmatrix} \hat{e}_1^T\hat{e}_1 & \cdots & \hat{e}_1^T\hat{e}_k \\ \vdots & & \\ \hat{e}_k^T\hat{e}_1 & \cdots & \hat{e}_k^T\hat{e}_k \end{bmatrix} \tag{3.46}$$

in which $\hat{e}_i$ is the vector of residuals obtained by use of $\hat{\beta}_i$ and $\hat{\gamma}$ in the ith commodity equation. [Note that $\hat{\beta}_k$ is obtained from (3.4d).]

Before discussing an operational procedure for computing $\hat{\boldsymbol{\beta}}$, $\hat{\gamma}$ and $\hat{\boldsymbol{\Omega}}^*$, it is useful to note that (3.45a) corresponds to (3.42b) which is an *identical regressors problem.* It follows (as we have already remarked above) that the Aitken estimator (3.45a) is numerically equivalent to the ordinary least squares estimator,[20]

$$\hat{\boldsymbol{\beta}}^{\circ} = [(z^*)^T z^*]^{-1}(z^*)^T w \tag{3.47}$$

which is just a matrix representation of the simple least-squares estimators (3.26).

All of the above suggests the following iterative procedure for locating stationary points of L. From some initial guesses or estimates of $\boldsymbol{\beta}$ and γ, and with (say) $\boldsymbol{\Omega}^*$ set equal to the identity matrix of order $(k-1)$, refinements are computed using (3.47), (3.45b), and (3.46), in that order. These new values are then substituted successively into (3.47), (3.45b), and (3.46) to yield new estimates of $\boldsymbol{\beta}$, γ, and $\boldsymbol{\Omega}^*$; and so on. This is basically a Gauss-Seidel search procedure.[21] If it converges, the point located will be one in which the first-order conditions all hold simultaneously; i.e., a stationary point of the likelihood surface. If statistically consistent starting values are used, then the consistency property is preserved during iteration (Slutzky's Theorem).[22] Thus if convergence is achieved from a consistent set of starting values, a consistent root of the likelihood equation (i.e., of the first-order conditions) has been found. But such a consistent root is unique,[23] and the estimate so obtained is *the* maximum-likelihood estimate.

Solari warns that convergence with the Gauss-Seidel (or iterative Aitken) procedure can be slow.[24] Recent experience gives added force to this warning.[25]

More efficient search techniques require hill-climbing approaches in the spirit of the original Cowles Foundation procedures for computing full-information maximum-likelihood estimators for the structural form of a

---

[20] Zellner, "An Efficient Method . . .," op. cit.

[21] S. M. Goldfeld and R. E. Quandt, *Non-Linear Methods in Econometrics* (Amsterdam and London: North-Holland, 1972), pp. 17–18.

[22] Phoebus Dhrymes, *Econometrics: Statistical Foundations and Applications* (New York: Harper & Row), p. 111.

[23] Ibid., pp. 117–120.

[24] Solari, "Sur L'Estimation du Systeme Lineaire . . .," op. cit., p. 9.

[25] Experience at the Development Research Center of the World Bank indicates that an efficient Gauss-Seidel search was of the order of 40 *times* slower than the gradient methods used by Carlevaro and Rossier in LINEX.

Table 3–3

Stone's Linear Expenditure System Fitted to Australian Data, 1948–1949 through 1966–1967: Principal Results of Maximum Likelihood Fit

	Estimates of					
Commodity Group i	Marginal Budget Share β_i	Total Expenditure Elasticity[a, e] E_i	Stone-Geary Parameter[b] γ_i	Own Price Elasticity[a] η_{ii}	Quasi-R^2 [d]	Durbin-Watson Statistic
1. Food	.1043	0.40565	222.16	−0.17756	.9957	.850
2. Tobacco and drink	.0644	0.59843	93.37	−0.17732	.9904	.624
3. Clothing	.0463	0.35724	100.93	−0.11503	.9167	.730
4. Household durables	.1213	1.45805	48.23	−0.37967	.9777	.873
5. Housing	.1936	2.06527	71.48	−0.52941	.9953	1.545
6. Fuel	.0480	1.80847	16.57	−0.39518	.9452	.640
7. Private transportation	.2038	2.38555	48.57	−0.58679	.9512	1.457
8. Services	.1894	1.36315	104.81	−0.41222	.9974	1.360
9. Other	.0288	0.37057	78.87	−0.10133	.9732	1.608
Sum	1.000		784.99[c]			

[a] Evaluated at sample mean values of average budget shares.
[b] Units are Australian dollars at prices of 1966–1967 (per capita).
[c] Units are Australian dollars of 1966–1967 purchasing power (per capita).
[d] $1 - \left(\sum_{t=1}^{N} \hat{u}_{it}^2 \Big/ \sum_{t=1}^{N} v_{it}^2 \right)$.
[e] "Total Expenditure" excludes Public Transportation.

simultaneous equations system.[26] Modern software capabilities allow such a search to be carried out on the basis either of an analytically specified Hessian of L, or via a computational evaluation of these second derivatives by a differencing method.[27] A detailed discussion of efficient computational procedures for the location of the extrema of a nonlinear function, however, would carry us well beyond the scope of this book.

Maximum-likelihood results obtained using LINEX are reported in Tables 3–3 and 3–4. The data are basically the same as those for Table 3–2, except that total expenditure has been redefined net of Public Transportation, and the deletion of this commodity from the system has made it possible to disaggregate the Fuel category from the previous Housing and Fuel category.[28] The reason for deleting Public Transportation is that the *invariance theorems* concerning the deletion of an arbitrarily chosen equation prior to estimation all assume that the domain of $\boldsymbol{\beta}$ is unrestricted, whereas LINEX searches only in the non-negative half-space. Corner solutions such as that obtained for Public Transportation in the systems LS approach consequently would lead to a loss of uniqueness of the estimates of the remaining coefficients. The starting values used in the ML search were obtained from a systems LS search of the type described above. The LS search took 42 iterations. The ML estimates were obtained using LINEX after only six additional iterations.

The asymptotic variances and covariances of the MLE's are obtained in the usual manner by evaluating the Hessian of the (log) likelihood function at the ML solution values of the parameters. The Hessian is

$$\underset{(2k-1)\times(2k-1)}{\mathbf{L}} = \left[\begin{array}{c:c} \dfrac{\partial^2 L}{\partial(\boldsymbol{\beta}^\circ)^2} & \dfrac{\partial^2 L}{(\partial\boldsymbol{\beta}^\circ\,\partial\boldsymbol{\gamma})} \\ \hdashline \left[\dfrac{\partial^2 L}{(\partial\boldsymbol{\beta}^\circ\,\partial\boldsymbol{\gamma})}\right]^T & \dfrac{\partial^2 L}{(\partial\boldsymbol{\gamma}^2)} \end{array}\right] \tag{3.48}$$

in which, for example, $\partial^2 L/[\partial(\boldsymbol{\beta}^\circ)^2]$ is the $(k-1)$-order square matrix whose (i, j)th element is $\partial^2 L/(\partial\beta_i\,\partial\beta_j)$, and in which $[\partial^2 L/(\partial\boldsymbol{\beta}^\circ\,\partial\boldsymbol{\gamma})]$ is the $(k-1)\times k$ matrix whose (i, j)th element is $\partial^2 L/(\partial\beta_i\,\partial\gamma_j)$. The block diagonal terms of (3.48) may be worked out readily from the partially linear representations

[26] T. C. Koopmans, H. Rubin, and R. B. Leipnik, "Measuring the Equation Systems of Dynamic Economics," in T. C. Koopmans, Ed., *Statistical Inference in Dynamic Economic Models* (New York: Wiley, 1950), Cowles Foundation Monograph No. 10, pp. 53–237.

[27] See, for example, Y. Bard, "Nonlinear Parameter Estimation and Programming," I.B.M. Contributed Program Library 360D–13.6.003 (December 1967).

[28] The version of LINEX available to the author catered for a maximum of $k = 9$ commodities.

Table 3–4

Elasticity Estimates Based on Maximum-Likelihood Fit of Linear Expenditure System to Australian Data, 1948–1949 to 1966–1967

Elasticity of Consumption of		Elasticity with respect to the Price of the Commodity whose ID Number[a] is: 1	2	3	4	5	6	7	8	9	Total Expenditure[b]
1. Food	U	−0.17756	−0.03840	−0.04883	−0.02383	−0.02219	−0.00684	−0.01798	−0.04087	−0.02913	0.40565
	C	−0.07326	0.00527	0.00379	0.00993	0.01583	0.00393	0.01667	0.01549	0.00235	
2. Tobacco and	U	−0.14128	−0.17732	−0.07203	−0.03516	−0.03273	−0.01010	−0.02653	−0.06030	−0.04298	0.59843
drink	C	0.01259	−0.11290	0.00559	0.01464	0.02336	0.00580	0.02459	0.02286	0.00347	
3. Clothing	U	−0.08434	−0.03382	−0.11503	−0.02099	−0.01954	−0.00603	−0.01584	−0.03600	−0.02565	0.35724
	C	0.00751	0.00464	−0.06870	0.00874	0.01394	0.00346	0.01468	0.01364	0.00207	
4. Household	U	−0.34423	−0.13802	−0.17550	−0.37967	−0.07975	−0.02460	−0.06464	−0.14692	−0.10471	1.45805
durables	C	0.03066	0.01894	0.01362	−0.25833	0.05692	0.01412	0.05992	0.05569	0.00846	
5. Housing	U	−0.48759	−0.19550	−0.24859	−0.12134	−0.52941	−0.03485	−0.09157	−0.20810	−0.14831	2.06527
	C	0.04344	0.02683	0.01930	0.05053	−0.33583	0.02000	0.08487	0.07888	0.01198	
6. Fuel	U	−0.42696	−0.17119	−0.21768	−0.10626	−0.09892	−0.39518	−0.08018	−0.18223	−0.12987	1.80847
	C	0.03803	0.02349	0.01690	0.04425	0.07059	−0.34715	0.07432	0.06907	0.01049	
7. Private	U	−0.56320	−0.22582	−0.28715	−0.14016	−0.13049	−0.04025	−0.58679	−0.24037	−0.17131	2.38555
transportation	C	0.05017	0.03099	0.02229	0.05837	0.09312	0.02310	−0.38299	0.09112	0.01383	
8. Services	U	−0.32182	−0.12904	−0.16408	−0.08009	−0.07456	−0.02300	−0.06044	−0.41222	−0.09789	1.36315
	C	0.02867	0.01771	0.01274	0.03335	0.05321	0.01320	0.05602	−0.22280	0.00791	
9. Other	U	−0.08749	−0.03508	−0.04460	−0.02177	−0.02027	−0.00625	−0.01643	−0.03734	−0.10133	0.37057
	C	0.00779	0.00481	0.00346	0.00907	0.01447	0.00359	0.01523	0.01415	−0.07257	

[a] All elasticities are evaluated at sample mean values of average budget shares and prices.
[b] Excludes Public transportation.
U Ordinary (uncompensated) elasticity. Row total = negative of total expenditure elasticity.
C Compensated elasticity. Row total = 0.

(3.42b) and (3.43b) of the LES. These are

$$\underset{(k-1)\times(k-1)}{\frac{\partial^2 L}{\partial(\boldsymbol{\beta}^\circ)^2}} = -(\boldsymbol{z}^*)^T[(\boldsymbol{\Omega}^*)^{-1} \otimes \boldsymbol{I}_N]\boldsymbol{z}^* \tag{3.49}$$

and

$$\frac{\partial^2 L}{\partial(\boldsymbol{\gamma})^2} = -(\boldsymbol{Z}^*)^T[(\boldsymbol{\Omega}^*)^{-1} \otimes \boldsymbol{I}_N]\boldsymbol{Z}^* \tag{3.50}$$

The off-diagonal terms are more difficult (since the dependence of $\boldsymbol{z}^*$ on $\boldsymbol{\gamma}$ and $\boldsymbol{Z}$ on $\boldsymbol{\beta}^\circ$ have to be taken into account). Keep in mind that

$$\frac{\partial L}{\partial \boldsymbol{\beta}^\circ} = (\boldsymbol{z}^*)^T \boldsymbol{A}(\boldsymbol{w} - \boldsymbol{z}^*\boldsymbol{\beta}^\circ) \tag{3.51a}$$

$$= (\boldsymbol{z}^*)^T \boldsymbol{A}(\boldsymbol{W} - \boldsymbol{Z}^*\boldsymbol{\gamma})$$

and that

$$\frac{\partial L}{\partial \boldsymbol{\gamma}} = (\boldsymbol{Z}^*)^T \boldsymbol{A}(\boldsymbol{W} - \boldsymbol{Z}^*\boldsymbol{\gamma}) \tag{3.51b}$$

$$= (\boldsymbol{Z}^*)^T \boldsymbol{A}(\boldsymbol{w} - \boldsymbol{z}^*\boldsymbol{\beta}^\circ)$$

in which

$$\boldsymbol{A} = (\boldsymbol{\Omega}^*)^{-1} \otimes \boldsymbol{I}_N \tag{3.51c}$$

In the second line of (3.51a) only $\boldsymbol{z}^*$ is a function of $\boldsymbol{\gamma}$ (apart from $\boldsymbol{\gamma}$ itself). If $\boldsymbol{B}$ is any matrix with typical element b_{ij}, let us agree that by $\partial \boldsymbol{B}/\partial \gamma_l$ we mean the matrix of similar dimensions whose typical element is $\partial b_{ij}/\partial \gamma_l$. Differentiating (3.51a) with respect to γ_l, we obtain

$$\frac{\partial^2 L}{(\partial \boldsymbol{\beta}^\circ \partial \gamma_l)} = \left[\frac{\partial \boldsymbol{z}^*}{\partial \gamma_l}\right]^T \boldsymbol{A}\boldsymbol{W} - \frac{\partial}{\partial \gamma_l}\{(\boldsymbol{z}^*)^T \boldsymbol{A}\boldsymbol{Z}^*\boldsymbol{\gamma}\} \tag{3.52}$$

But

$$\boldsymbol{z}^* = \boldsymbol{I}_{k-1} \otimes \boldsymbol{z} \tag{3.53}$$

hence

$$\frac{\partial \boldsymbol{z}^*}{\partial \gamma_l} = \boldsymbol{I}_{k-1} \otimes \frac{\partial \boldsymbol{z}}{\partial \gamma_l} \tag{3.54}$$

But, from (3.38a),

$$z = m - P\gamma \tag{3.55}$$

Hence

$$\frac{\partial z}{\partial \gamma_l} = -p^l \tag{3.56}$$

that is, the $N \times 1$ vector of derivatives of "supernumerary expenditure" expenditures with respect to γ_l is the negative of the observation vector on the lth price.

Working now on the second right-hand term of (3.52), the product rule of differentiation yields

$$\frac{\partial}{\partial \gamma_l}\{(z^*)^T A Z^* \gamma\} = (z^*)^T A Z^* \frac{\partial \gamma}{\partial \gamma_l} + \left[\frac{\partial (z^*)}{\partial \gamma_l}\right]^T A Z^* \gamma \tag{3.57}$$

But $\partial\gamma/\partial\gamma_l$ is just the lth unit vector of order k, having zeros everywhere except the lth position. Let the lth unit vector of order k be written ι_l. Then, using (3.54), (3.56), and (3.57) in (3.52), we have

$$\frac{\partial^2 L}{(\partial \beta^\circ \, \partial \gamma_l)} = [I_{k-1} \otimes -p^l]^T A(W - Z^*\gamma) - (z^*)^T A Z^* \iota_l \quad (l = 1, \ldots, k) \tag{3.58}$$

which is a vector of $(k-1)$ elements. The $(k-1) \times k$ matrix of derivatives, $\partial^2 L/(\partial\beta^\circ \, \partial\gamma)$, is obtained by collecting these columns.[29]

Asymptotic variances and covariances are estimated by $-\hat{L}^{-1}$, in which the "hat" on L indicates that the MLE's of γ, β, and Ω^* have to be inserted into (3.49), (3.50), and (3.58) in order to allow evaluation of the Hessian. In the case of the system estimated in Table 3–3, estimates of asymptotic variances and covariances are shown in Table 3–5. Approximate tests of significance based on large sample theory may be made using ratios of estimated coefficients to estimated asymptotic standard deviations. In the case of the deleted kth equation, the asymptotic variance of $\hat{\beta}_k$ (where $\hat{\beta}_k$ by definition is one minus the sum of the elements of $\hat{\beta}^\circ$) may be found from

$$\operatorname{var}(\hat{\beta}_k) = \mathbf{1}^T \, \mathbf{var}(\hat{\beta}^\circ)\mathbf{1} \tag{3.59}$$

in which $\mathbf{1}$ is a vector of $(k-1)$ units, and $\mathbf{var}(\hat{\beta}^\circ)$ is the $(k-1) \times (k-1)$ asymptotic variance covariance matrix in the first part of Table 3–5.

[29] No convenient compact representation of the collected columns seems to be available without using some nonstandard matrix operations.

Table 3–5

Estimated Asymptotic Variance-Covariance Matrix for Linear Expenditure System Results of Table 3–3

1. Variance-Covariance Matrix for $\hat{\gamma}$

	γ_1	γ_2	γ_3	γ_4	γ_5	γ_6	γ_7	γ_8	γ_9
γ_1	26.80	14.45	12.63	20.16	86.38	8.78	40.44	49.90	12.38
γ_2	14.45	15.07	4.24	16.59	64.69	7.94	39.06	36.45	7.70
γ_3	12.63	4.24	11.62	8.04	29.44	2.23	10.10	19.63	7.88
γ_4	20.16	16.59	8.04	22.76	81.35	9.96	47.57	45.59	10.70
γ_5	86.38	64.69	29.44	81.35	351.98	39.25	192.62	194.28	38.06
γ_6	8.78	7.94	2.23	9.96	39.25	5.46	21.96	20.83	3.32
γ_7	40.44	39.06	10.10	47.57	192.62	21.96	136.39	106.98	19.64
γ_8	49.90	36.45	19.63	45.59	194.28	20.83	106.98	110.46	22.92
γ_9	12.38	7.70	7.88	10.70	38.06	3.32	19.64	22.92	14.06

2. Variance-Covariance Matrix for $\hat{\beta}$

	β_1	β_2	β_3	β_4	β_5	β_6	β_7	β_8	β_9
β_1	0.00012563	−0.00003699	0.00010155	0.00001186	−0.00010231	−0.00000409	−0.00014771	0.00003784	0.00001422
β_2	−0.00003699	0.00004923	−0.00004579	0.00001921	−0.00002441	0.00001555	0.00003898	−0.00000379	−0.00001200
β_3	0.00010155	−0.00004579	0.00020177	0.00001163	−0.00013884	−0.00002749	−0.00018234	0.00001703	0.00006247
β_4	0.00001186	0.00001921	0.00001163	0.00011328	−0.00019821	0.00003475	0.00003583	−0.00001326	−0.00001509
β_5	−0.00010231	−0.00002441	−0.00013884	−0.00019821	0.00068001	−0.00003459	−0.00013926	−0.00001614	−0.00002625
β_6	−0.00000409	0.00001555	−0.00002749	0.00003475	−0.00003459	0.00003281	0.00001996	−0.00000348	−0.00003342
β_7	−0.00014771	0.00003898	−0.00018234	0.00003583	−0.00013926	0.00001996	0.00050873	−0.00003446	−0.00009972
β_8	0.00003784	−0.00000379	0.00001703	−0.00001326	−0.00001614	−0.00000348	−0.00003446	0.00004768	−0.00003142
β_9	0.00001422	−0.00001200	0.00006247	−0.00001509	−0.00002625	−0.00003342	−0.00009972	−0.00003142	0.00014122

3. Cross Covariances for $\hat{\beta}$ and $\hat{\gamma}$

	γ_1	γ_2	γ_3	γ_4	γ_5	γ_6	γ_7	γ_8	γ_9
β_1	0.0009	0.0253	−0.0085	0.0251	0.0862	0.0130	0.0864	0.0435	0.0051
β_2	0.0116	−0.0080	0.0103	0.0006	0.0152	−0.0014	−0.0001	0.0085	0.0040
β_3	−0.0059	0.0192	−0.0320	0.0129	0.0679	0.0122	0.0685	0.0248	−0.0098
β_4	0.0373	0.0220	0.0140	0.0207	0.1399	0.0112	0.0743	0.0801	0.0162
β_5	−0.1070	−0.0784	−0.0255	−0.0954	−0.4613	−0.0517	−0.2331	−0.2449	−0.0339
β_6	0.0153	0.0062	0.0111	0.0086	0.0416	0.0000	0.0255	0.0289	0.0123
β_7	0.0585	0.0100	0.0464	0.0222	0.0985	0.0087	−0.0517	0.0619	0.0323
β_8	0.0057	0.0097	0.0021	0.0162	0.0349	0.0070	0.0354	0.0158	0.0117
β_9	−0.0163	−0.0060	−0.0179	−0.0109	−0.0229	0.0009	−0.0052	−0.0185	−0.0380

3.4 Variants on the LES

3.4.1 The LES Under Habit Formation (Pollak and Wales)

In the formulation of Stone's LES discussed above, the utility function is stationary. For the analysis of time-series data, this may be too rigid a view. If patterns of national demand are under study, and the set of parameters $\boldsymbol{\gamma}$ are interpreted as "minimum socially acceptable consumption requirements," some provision for growth in this minimum over time would seem to be needed. One option, implemented by Stone, is to write a linear trend into the gammas;[30] another, suggested by Stone and followed up by Pollak and Wales, is the use of lagged consumption as a determinant of the effective origin $\boldsymbol{\gamma}$ of the utility map.[31] In both cases we write the utility function as

$$u_t(\boldsymbol{x}_t) = \sum_{i=1}^{k} \beta_i \log(x_{it} - \gamma_{it}) \tag{3.60}$$

To embody the *habit formation* hypothesis, we write

$$\gamma_{it} = \gamma_i^* + \lambda_i x_{it-1} \tag{3.61}$$

in which the coefficient of habit formation λ_i should not be confused with the marginal utility of expenditure, λ, of Chapter 1.[32] In this new formulation, the number of "free" parameters is $(3k-1)$; namely, $\boldsymbol{\beta}^\circ$, $\boldsymbol{\gamma}^* = (\gamma_1^*, \ldots, \gamma_k^*)^T$, and $\boldsymbol{\lambda} = (\lambda_1, \ldots, \lambda_k)^T$. Under this formulation a stationary representation of the utility index exists, provided *past* consumption as well as present consumption is admitted as an argument of the utility function. Thus

$$\begin{aligned} u_t(\boldsymbol{x}_t) &= u^*(\boldsymbol{x}_t, \boldsymbol{x}_{t-1}, \boldsymbol{x}_{t-2}, \ldots) \\ &= \sum_{i=1}^{k} \beta_i \log(x_{it} - \gamma_i^* - \lambda_i x_{it-1}) \end{aligned} \tag{3.62}$$

---

[30] Stone, "Linear Expenditure Systems and Demand Analysis," op. cit., p. 522.

[31] A. Brown, Richard Stone, and D. A. Rowe, "Demand Analysis and Projections for Britain, 1900–1970: A Study in Method," in J. Sandee, Ed., *Europe's Future Consumption*, Vol. 2 (Amsterdam: North-Holland, 1964), pp. 200–225. Robert A. Pollak and Terence J. Wales, "Estimation of the Linear Expenditure System," *Econometrica* 37, no. 4 (October 1969): 611–628.

[32] Pollak and Wales, ibid., consider three other variants of habit formation: (i) proportional habit formation, in which all γ_i^* are set to zero a priori; (ii) two variants based on rates of consumption in the past.

The maximization of (3.62) at any given t subject to the budget constraint, of course, gives us the LES under habit formation; namely,

$$v_{it} \equiv p_{it} x_{it} = p_i \gamma_{it} + \beta_i (m_t - \mathbf{p}_t^T \gamma_t) \qquad (i = 1, \ldots, k) \qquad (3.63a)$$

with

$$\gamma_t = \gamma^* + \boldsymbol{\lambda}^{\text{diag}} \mathbf{x}_{t-1} \qquad (3.63b)$$

in which $\boldsymbol{\lambda}^{\text{diag}}$ is the diagonal matrix formed from the vector $\boldsymbol{\lambda}$.

The estimation (3.63a and b) depends critically on the stochastic specification. Pollak and Wales add a zero mean error term to the *demand* functions.[33] Also, they postulate that the covariance matrix of these disturbances should be unaffected by proportional changes in prices and total expenditure (which is a type of generalization of the homogeneity requirement in demand analysis). The full demand system (including its stochastic part) is written

$$x_{it} = \gamma_{it} + \frac{\beta_i}{p_{it}} (m_t - \mathbf{p}_t^T \gamma_t) + e_{it}^* \qquad (i = 1, \ldots, k) \qquad (3.64)$$

in which the e_{it}^* all have zero expectation. This is equivalent to specifying a stochastic γ_t, which can be seen as follows. Instead of (3.63b), write

$$\gamma_t^\circ = \gamma^* + \boldsymbol{\lambda}^{\text{diag}} \mathbf{x}_{t-1} \qquad (3.65)$$

which will leave the symbol γ_{it} free for redefinition as follows,

$$\gamma_{it} = \gamma_{it}^\circ + e_{it}^\circ \qquad (3.66)$$

in which e_{it}° is a zero-mean stochastic variable. Substituting from (3.66) into (3.63a), and dividing by the ith price, we obtain

$$x_{it} = \gamma_{it}^\circ + \frac{\beta_i}{p_{it}} (m_t - \mathbf{p}_t^T \gamma_t^\circ) + \left(e_{it}^\circ - \frac{\beta_i}{p_{it}} \sum_{j=1}^{k} p_{jt} e_{jt}^\circ \right) \qquad (i = 1, \ldots, k) \quad (3.67)$$

which, after appropriate notational adjustments, is equivalent to (3.64).[34] Pollak and Wales explore maximum likelihood methods for the estimation of (3.67) under the assumption that the errors $\{e_{it}^\circ\}$ are zero mean multivariate normal, with zero own- and cross-lag covariances, and with zero contemporaneous covariances. The variances of the e_{it}°'s are alternatively specified

[33] Ibid., pp. 615–616.

[34] From here on we will write the last term in parentheses on the right of (3.67) as e_{it}^*. In (3.67) γ_t° is the k-element vector with typical element γ_{it}°.

either as

$$E(e_{it}^{\circ})^2 = \sigma_i^2 \qquad \text{(all } t) \tag{3.68a}$$

or

$$E(e_{it}^{\circ})^2 \propto E(x_{it}^2 \mid \boldsymbol{p}_t; m_t) \tag{3.68b}$$

As in all versions of the LES, singular covariance matrices are encountered, so that an equation has to be dropped from the system prior to estimation.[35]

After this truncation, the transformation relating the stochastic part e_{it}° of minimal consumption requirements to the error e_{it}^{*} in the final form (3.67) of the demand system is

$$\boldsymbol{e}_t^* = \boldsymbol{M}_t \boldsymbol{e}_t^{\circ} \tag{3.69}$$

in which $\boldsymbol{e}_t^*$ and $\boldsymbol{e}_t^{\circ}$ are $(k-1)$-order vectors with typical elements e_{it}^* and e_{it}° respectively; whilst $\boldsymbol{M}_t$ is the nonsingular $(k-1)$-order square matrix,

$$\boldsymbol{M}_t = \begin{bmatrix} (1-\beta_1) & \dfrac{-\beta_1 p_{2t}}{p_{1t}} & \cdots & \dfrac{-\beta_1 p_{k-1,t}}{p_{1t}} \\ \dfrac{-\beta_2 p_{1t}}{p_{2t}} & (1-\beta_2) & \cdots & \dfrac{-\beta_2 p_{k-1,t}}{p_{2t}} \\ \vdots & \vdots & & \vdots \\ \dfrac{-\beta_{k-1} p_{1t}}{p_{k-1,t}} & \dfrac{-\beta_{k-1} p_{2t}}{p_{k-1,t}} & \cdots & (1-\beta_{k-1}) \end{bmatrix} \tag{3.70}$$

From any given specialization of the variance-covariance matrix of the e_{it}°'s, the corresponding covariance structure of the e_{it}^{*}'s may be determined. If, in general,

$$E[\boldsymbol{e}_t^{\circ}(\boldsymbol{e}_t^{\circ})^T] = \boldsymbol{\Sigma}_t \tag{3.71}$$

then

$$E[\boldsymbol{e}_t^{*}(\boldsymbol{e}_t^{*})^T] = \boldsymbol{M}_t \boldsymbol{\Sigma}_t \boldsymbol{M}_t^T \tag{3.72}$$

$$= \boldsymbol{Q}_t \qquad \text{(say)}$$

[35] The assumption that *all* contemporaneous covariances vanish is untenable in light of the aggregation requirement

$$\textstyle\sum_{i=1}^{k} p_{it} e_{it}^* \equiv 0$$

After an equation has been deleted from the system, however, there is no theoretical necessity for remaining covariances to be nonzero. See L. Solari, "Sur L'Estimation du Systeme Lineaire de Depenses," op. cit., p. 7.

The log likelihood function for the system is,

$$L = \frac{-(k-1)N}{2}\log(2\pi) - \frac{1}{2}\sum_{t=1}^{N}[\log|\boldsymbol{Q}_t| + (\boldsymbol{e}_t^*)^T\boldsymbol{Q}_t^{-1}\boldsymbol{e}_t^*] \tag{3.73}$$

$$= \frac{-(k-1)N}{2}\log(2\pi) - \sum_{t=1}^{N}\log|\boldsymbol{M}_t| - \frac{1}{2}\sum_{t=1}^{N}[\log|\boldsymbol{\Sigma}_t| + (\boldsymbol{e}_t^\circ)^T\boldsymbol{\Sigma}_t^{-1}\boldsymbol{e}_t^\circ]$$

Pollak and Wales report the results of maximizing (3.73) with respect to the parameters $\boldsymbol{\beta}^\circ$, γ^*, $\boldsymbol{\lambda}$, and $\boldsymbol{\sigma}^2 = (\sigma_1^2, \ldots, \sigma_{k-1}^2)$. The computer program they used was "Grad x," developed by Goldfeld, Quandt, and Trotter. Numerical first and second derivatives were used, according to Pollak and Wales, because "they permit estimation of variants of the basic model without substantial

Table 3–6

Linear Expenditure System Under Habit Formation: Pollak and Wales' Results for U.S.A., 1948–1965

Parameter		Commodity			
		Food	Clothing	Shelter	Other
Marginal budget share	β_i	.348	.219	.302	.130
Subsistence coefficient[a]	γ_i^*	136	49	59	23
Coefficient of habit formation	λ_i	.749	.797	.928	.939
Variance	σ_i^2	1.21	2.34	.35	.49
Coefficient of multiple determination	R^2	.96	.93	.99	.99

SOURCE: Robert A. Pollak and Terence J. Wales, "Estimation of the Linear Expenditure System," *Econometrica* 37, no. 4 (October 1969): 621.
[a] Expressed in U.S. dollars of 1958.

reprogramming." The authors also claim that the numerical approach to taking derivatives reduces computation time (although it is not clear that this would be so in every, or even in most applications).[36] Results obtained by Pollak and Wales using these methods are given in Table 3–6. The variance assumption underlying the results reproduced is (3.68b). The authors comment that "the model is not acceptable because calculated [γ_{it}] values exceed the corresponding consumption values in every time period for all goods."[37]

[36] Pollak and Wales, op. cit., p. 628.

[37] Ibid., p. 622.

Recently the work of Pollak and Wales has been generalized by Phlips to make the γ_i's dependent on state variables which may be interpreted either as the accumulated strength of a habit (in the case of consumables) or as an inventory (in the case of durables).[38]

3.4.2 Triad Restrictions Only[39]

In the linear expenditure system of Stone, there is a 1:1 correspondence between the market behavioral relations and the constrained maximum problem. Such correspondence is global. Thus, at any set of values of the exogenous variables (total expenditure, prices) and the corresponding values of the endogenous variables (commodity expenditures), the system conforms to the properties of additivity, homogeneity, and symmetry. We now consider systems in which a linear form for the expenditure equations is taken to be an adequate *approximation* to the behavioral relations in the region encompassing the data. Various restrictions on the form of the utility function are considered in turn.

We note that global homogeneity can easily be achieved in a linear expenditure system simply by setting all of the constants in (3.3) to zero.[40] This we shall do. If we require in addition that the expenditure system is *globally* additive, then necessary and sufficient conditions are

$$\sum_{i=1}^{k} \beta_i = 1 \tag{3.74a}$$

and

$$\sum_{i=1}^{k} a_{ij} \equiv 0 \qquad (\text{all } j = 1, \ldots, k) \tag{3.74b}$$

In this section we ask the following question: given that the additivity conditions (3.74a) and (3.74b), as well as homogeneity, are global requirements, what additional constraints are placed on the parameters $\{a_{ij};\, \beta_i\}$ of a linear expenditure system by *local* enforcement of *symmetry*? In particular, if the latter property is required to hold at coordinates $\{\boldsymbol{p}^\circ, m^\circ\}$, what transformations of the data lead to an efficient format for estimation of a (locally) linear expenditure system?

---

[38] Louis Phlips, "A Dynamic Version of the Linear Expenditure System," *Review of Economics and Statistics* 54, no. 4 (November 1972): 450–458.

[39] I am grateful to Tran Van Hoa who provided the computations reported in this section.

[40] "Homogeneity" in this discussion always means homogeneity (of degree zero) of the underlying demand functions.

3.4.2.1 Leser's Transformation. It is helpful to start with a transformation that seems to have been suggested first by Leser.[41] Let $\{\boldsymbol{x}^\circ\}$ and $\{\boldsymbol{v}^\circ\}$ be the quantity and expenditure vectors which correspond to $\{\boldsymbol{p}^\circ; m^\circ\}$. (The latter may be, say, sample mean values.) Let $\{\sigma_{ij}^\circ\}$ be the set of partial substitution elasticities evaluated at this set of coordinates. Let the average budget shares at this coordinate set be

$$w_i^\circ = \left(\frac{p_i^\circ x_i^\circ}{m^\circ}\right) \tag{3.75}$$

in which the variable w_i° should not be confused with the quite different variable w_{it} of (3.19) and (3.42). We have from (1.47),

$$\sigma_{ij}^\circ = \frac{\varepsilon_{ij}^\circ}{w_j^\circ} \tag{3.76}$$

where ε_{ij}° is the income-compensated cross-price elasticity of the consumption of i with respect to the price of j, and superscript degree signs indicate evaluation at the coordinate set $\{\boldsymbol{p}^\circ; m^\circ\}$. The *fundamental equation of value theory*, from (1.13), tells us that

$$\varepsilon_{ij}^\circ = \frac{\partial x_i^\circ}{\partial p_j^\circ}\frac{p_j^\circ}{x_i^\circ} + \frac{x_j^\circ}{x_i^\circ}\frac{\partial x_i^\circ}{\partial m^\circ}p_j^\circ \tag{3.77}$$

$$= \eta_{ij}^\circ + \frac{v_j^\circ(\partial x_i^\circ/\partial m^\circ)}{x_i^\circ} \tag{3.78}$$

where η_{ij}° is the ordinary cross elasticity of i with respect to j's price, and where all derivatives have been evaluated at the convenient coordinate set. (Thus $\partial x_i^\circ/\partial m^\circ$ is shorthand for $\partial x_i/\partial m$ evaluated at $x_i = x_i^\circ$ and $m = m^\circ$.) To examine what equations (3.77) and (3.78) imply for the linear expenditure system, we differentiate (3.3) partially, first with respect to m, and then with respect to p_j.

$$\frac{\partial v_i}{\partial m} = p_i\frac{\partial x_i}{\partial m} = \beta_i \tag{3.79}$$

hence

$$\frac{\partial x_i}{\partial m} = \frac{\beta_i}{p_i} \tag{3.80}$$

[41] C. E. V. Leser, "The Pattern of Australian Demand," *Economic Record* 34 (1958): 212–222; "Demand Functions for Nine Commodity Groups in Australia," *Australian Journal of Statistics* 2, no. 3 (November 1960): 102–113; "Commodity Group Expenditure Functions for the United Kingdom, 1948–57," *Econometrica* 29, no. 1 (January 1961): 24–32.

in particular

$$\frac{\partial x_i^\circ}{\partial m^\circ} = \frac{\beta_i}{p_i^\circ} \qquad (i = 1, \ldots, k) \tag{3.81}$$

The partial price derivatives of expenditures $v_i \equiv p_i x_i$ are

$$\frac{\partial v_i}{\partial p_j} = \frac{\partial (p_i x_i)}{\partial p_j} \tag{3.82}$$

$$= p_i \frac{\partial x_i}{\partial p_j} \qquad (\text{when } i \neq j) \tag{3.83}$$

$$= p_i \frac{\partial x_i}{\partial p_i} + x_i \qquad (\text{when } i = j) \tag{3.84}$$

Extending the differentiation to the RHS of (3.3), and again evaluating derivatives at the convenient coordinate set, we obtain

$$p_i^\circ \frac{\partial x_i^\circ}{\partial p_j^\circ} = a_{ij} \qquad (\text{when } i \neq j) \tag{3.85}$$

$$p_i^\circ \frac{\partial x_i^\circ}{\partial p_i^\circ} + x_i^\circ = a_{ii} \qquad (\text{when } i = j) \tag{3.86}$$

Equations (3.85) and (3.86) enable us to write (3.78) as

$$\varepsilon_{ij}^\circ = p_j^\circ \frac{a_{ij}}{p_i^\circ x_i^\circ} + \beta_i x_j^\circ \frac{p_j^\circ}{p_i^\circ x_i^\circ} \qquad (\text{when } i \neq j) \tag{3.87}$$

Substituting from (3.87) into (3.76), we obtain

$$\sigma_{ij}^\circ = p_j^\circ \frac{a_{ij}}{v_i^\circ w_j^\circ} + \beta_i \frac{v_j^\circ}{v_i^\circ w_j^\circ} \qquad (\text{when } i \neq j) \tag{3.88}$$

whence

$$a_{ij} = v_i^\circ w_j^\circ \frac{\sigma_{ij}^\circ}{p_j^\circ} - \beta_i \frac{v_i^\circ}{p_j^\circ} \qquad (\text{for } i \neq j) \tag{3.89}$$

The last of these equations is the first part of the transformation suggested by Leser.[42]

---

[42] Leser, "Demand Functions for Nine Commodity Groups," op. cit., p. 105.

Homogeneity, we have seen, implies that

$$\sum_{j=1}^{k} \frac{(dx_i)}{(dp_j)} p_j \equiv \sum_{j=1}^{k} \kappa_{ij} p_j \equiv 0 \qquad \text{for all } i \tag{3.90}$$

where the notation follows Chapter 1. (Thus, $(d*)/(d**)$ is the income-compensated derivative of $(*)$ with respect to $(**)$.) Dividing each side of (3.90) by x_i, the resulting equation is

$$\sum_{j=1}^{k} \sigma_{ij} w_j = 0 \tag{3.91}$$

Rearranging, and evaluating at the convenient coordinate set, we obtain

$$\sigma_{ii}^{\circ} = -\left(\sum_{j \neq i}^{k} w_j^{\circ} \sigma_{ij}^{\circ}\right) \div w_i^{\circ} \tag{3.92}$$

where σ_{ii}° is the "own" substitution elasticity of the ith good. (Under the competitive market conditions assumed here, this own-substitution elasticity is proportional to the income-compensated elasticity of i with respect to its own price, the constant of proportionality being the reciprocal of i's average budget share, w_i°.)

In the matrix of price responses $A = [a_{ij}]$, the diagonal terms a_{ii} might be found in terms of the σ_{ij}°'s in either of two ways:

i. by enforcing global additivity; i.e., by invoking restriction (3.74b); or
ii. by examining the own-substitution effect, and using (3.92).

Fortunately, both approaches lead to the same result, namely that

$$a_{ii} = w_i v_i \sigma_{ii}^{\circ}/p_i^{\circ} + (1-\beta_i) v_i^{\circ}/p_i^{\circ} \tag{3.93}$$

Equations (3.92) and (3.93) may be combined as

$$a_{ij} = w_i^{\circ} v_j^{\circ} \sigma_{ij}^{\circ}/p_j^{\circ} - \beta_i v_j^{\circ}/p_j^{\circ} + \delta_{ij} v_i^{\circ}/p_i^{\circ} \tag{3.94}$$

where δ_{ij} is Kronecker's delta (i.e., $\delta_{ij} = 1$ when $i = j$, and equals 0 otherwise). Equation (3.94) is *Leser's approximately classical transformation* of a linear expenditure system.[43] The final step in this transformation procedure is to substitute back from (3.94) into (3.3), obtaining the linear expenditure system in terms of its new parameter set $\{\sigma_{ij}^{\circ}; \beta_i\}$. After some work we obtain

$$y_{it} = \sum_{j \neq i} \sigma_{ij}^{\circ} \zeta_{ijt} + \beta_i v_t \tag{3.95}$$

---

[43] Ibid.

in which

$$\zeta_{ijt} = w_i^\circ v_j^\circ (p_{jt}/p_j^\circ - p_{it}/p_i^\circ) \tag{3.96}$$

$$v_t = m_t - \sum_{j=1}^{m} x_j^\circ p_{jt} \tag{3.97}$$

and

$$y_{it} = v_{it} - p_{it} x_i^\circ \tag{3.98}$$

Equation (3.95) is the final operational form suggested by Leser.[44]

Let us take stock of what has been achieved. The linear expenditure system (3.3) was originally formulated in terms of k^2 price parameters, the a_{ij}'s. After invoking global additivity and homogeneity, there are $k(k-1)$ parameters left, the σ_{ij}°'s of (3.95). The *coup de grace* is given by calling up the Slutsky-Hicks symmetry property. If we require, in line with the theoretical ideas of Chapter 1, that $\sigma_{ij}^\circ = \sigma_{ji}^\circ$, then the price parameters are reduced to $\frac{1}{2}k(k-1)$ (which is just the number C_2^k of different pairs among k items).

3.4.2.2 Estimation Procedure.[45] There would be no point in estimating the transformation (3.95) on an equation-by-equation basis. For if we did so, there would be no guarantee that the σ_{ij}° value from fitting the ith equation would equal the σ_{ji}° value obtained by fitting the jth equation. But it has been the whole purpose of our exercise to exploit this equality in order to improve the efficiency of our estimates.

Two approaches are available for enforcing the pair-wise equality of the substitution elasticities, both of which are largely by-products of Zellner's classic paper on seemingly unrelated regressions.[46] In the first, all k equations are "stacked" one on top of the other to form one "super" regression equation. As all the parameters in the system are then all within one (super) equation, the theory for the estimation of an equation subject to constraints among its parameters becomes immediately relevant.[47] Variants of this approach have

---

[44] Ibid.

[45] The following section draws heavily on the Appendix of Powell, "Aitken Estimators . . .," op. cit., pp. 913–922.

[46] Zellner, "An Efficient Method of Estimating Seemingly Unrelated Regressions and Tests for Aggregation Bias," op. cit.

It is however true that Brandow had constructed and used "stacked regressions" preserving symmetry before the appearance of Zellner's paper. See G. E. Brandow, "Interrelations Among Demands for Farm Food Products and Implications for Control of Market Supply," *Pennsylvania Experiment Bulletin* 680, 1961.

[47] See A. S. Goldberger, *Econometric Theory* (New York: Wiley, 1964), pp. 256–259.

been explored theoretically and empirically by Byron and by Court.[48] The second alternative is equivalent, but reduces considerably the dimensions of an already formidable computational problem. In this approach, the constraints are built directly into the regressor matrices.[49] It is the latter alternative that we now explore.

Because combinational patterns are involved, to use a fully general notation at this stage would create, rather than solve, problems. Thus we will opt for a concrete problem which fully illustrates all that is involved, and from which the reader should have no difficulty generalizing. Specifically, let us examine a three-commodity model ($k = 3$). We restrict the number of commodities in this way because the complexity of the combinations we must handle increases with k: indeed, C_2^k gives a measure of this complexity, being the number of partial substitution elasticities σ_{ij} involved. We assume that the variables ζ_{ijt} of equation (3.96)—which are weighted differences of price relatives—have all been constructed, and shall denote observation vectors on these variables by $\boldsymbol{\zeta}_{ij}$. By $\boldsymbol{v}$ we shall mean the observation vector on supernumerary income—as defined in (3.97). The observation vector on transformed expenditure (y_{it}) on the ith commodity may be written $\boldsymbol{y}_i$. Then the ith transformed expenditure equation may be written

$$\underset{N\times 1}{\boldsymbol{y}_i} = \underset{N\times 1}{\boldsymbol{v}} \underset{1\times 1}{\beta_i} + \sum_{j\neq i}^{3} \underset{N\times 1}{\boldsymbol{\zeta}_{ij}} \underset{1\times 1}{\sigma_{ij}^{\circ}} + \underset{N\times 1}{\boldsymbol{e}_i} \qquad (i = 1, \ldots, 3) \tag{3.99}$$

where $\boldsymbol{e}_i$ is the observation vector on disturbances e_{it} which are assumed to enter (3.3) in an additive way.

These 3 equations may be "stacked" into one super equation as in (3.100).

$$\underset{3N\times 1}{\begin{bmatrix} \boldsymbol{y}_1 \\ \boldsymbol{y}_2 \\ \boldsymbol{y}_3 \end{bmatrix}} = \underset{3N\times 6}{\left[\begin{array}{ccc|ccc} \boldsymbol{v} & \boldsymbol{0} & \boldsymbol{0} & \boldsymbol{\zeta}_{12} & \boldsymbol{0} & \boldsymbol{\zeta}_{13} \\ \boldsymbol{0} & \boldsymbol{v} & \boldsymbol{0} & \boldsymbol{\zeta}_{21} & \boldsymbol{\zeta}_{23} & \boldsymbol{0} \\ \boldsymbol{0} & \boldsymbol{0} & \boldsymbol{v} & \boldsymbol{0} & \boldsymbol{\zeta}_{32} & \boldsymbol{\zeta}_{31} \end{array}\right]} \underset{6\times 1}{\begin{bmatrix} \beta_1 \\ \beta_2 \\ \beta_3 \\ \sigma_{12}^{\circ} \\ \sigma_{23}^{\circ} \\ \sigma_{13}^{\circ} \end{bmatrix}} + \underset{3N\times 1}{\begin{bmatrix} \boldsymbol{e}_1 \\ \boldsymbol{e}_2 \\ \boldsymbol{e}_3 \end{bmatrix}} \tag{3.100}$$

---

[48] R. P. Byron, "Methods for Estimating Demand Equations Using Prior Information: A Series of Experiments with Australian Data," *Australian Economic Papers* 7, no. 11 (December 1968): 227–248. R. H. Court, "Utility Maximization and the Demand for New Zealand Meats," *Econometrica* 35, nos. 3–4 (July–October 1967): 424–446.

[49] Powell, "Aitken Estimators . . .," op. cit.

Notice that the variables ζ_{ij} have been "juggled" on the RHS of the big regressor matrix in such a way that both ζ_{ij} and ζ_{ji} have the same regression coefficient, namely, σ_{ij}°. By this means the symmetry property is automatically built into the estimates. There are some complications involved, however, in estimation.

Following Zellner, the estimating procedure we shall apply is *Aitken's principle.*[50] Equation (3.100) (or the equivalent expressions for $k \neq 3$) can be written in a more compact notation as

$$y = X\beta + e \tag{3.101}$$

As we have seen, the contemporaneous covariance matrix of the disturbances $\boldsymbol{e}$ (namely, $\boldsymbol{\Omega}$), is singular.[51] As in the case of the LES of Stone, the operational procedure for estimation involves deletion of one equation (say the third). The truncated system is

$$\begin{bmatrix} y_1 \\ y_2 \end{bmatrix} = \left[\begin{array}{cc|ccc} v & 0 & \zeta_{12} & 0 & \zeta_{13} \\ 0 & v & \zeta_{21} & \zeta_{23} & 0 \end{array}\right] \begin{bmatrix} \beta_1 \\ \beta_2 \\ \sigma_{12}^{\circ} \\ \sigma_{23}^{\circ} \\ \sigma_{13}^{\circ} \end{bmatrix} + \begin{bmatrix} e_1 \\ e_2 \end{bmatrix} \tag{3.102}$$

For compactness, write this

$$y^* = X^*\beta^* + e^* \tag{3.103}$$

If the contemporaneous covariance matrix of this (full-rank) subsystem is $\boldsymbol{\Omega}^*$, then, ideally we would like to compute the Aitken estimator

$$\hat{\beta}^* = \{(X^*)^T[(\Omega^*)^{-1} \otimes I_N]X^*\}^{-1}(X^*)^T[(\Omega^*)^{-1} \otimes I_N]y^* \tag{3.104}$$

Because the covariance structure $\boldsymbol{\Omega}^*$ is unknown to us, however, equation (3.104) is not operational. First we must estimate $\boldsymbol{\Omega}^*$. An operational version of (3.104) may be obtained by substituting an estimate of $\boldsymbol{\Omega}^*$ for that unknown matrix. (The effect of such a substitution on the statistical properties of the estimator is mentioned below.) A logical starting point is the ordinary least-

---

[50] Arnold Zellner, "An Efficient Method of Estimating Seemingly Unrelated Regressions and Tests for Aggregation Bias," op. cit.

[51] We impose the same assumptions on the variances and covariances of the e_{it}'s as above; namely, that all own- and cross-lag covariances vanish.

squares estimator of (3.103). After fitting that equation by least squares we have available residuals $\hat{e}_1, \hat{e}_2, \ldots, \hat{e}_{k-1}$, which may be used as estimates of the e's. The contemporaneous covariances are estimated by

$$\hat{\omega}_{ij} = \frac{1}{N}\sum_{t=1}^{N} \hat{e}_{it}\,\hat{e}_{jt} \qquad (i = 1, \ldots, k-1) \tag{3.105}$$

When these elements of $\mathbf{\Omega}^*$ are substituted into (3.104), one obtains the Aitken-Zellner two-stage estimator.[52] If the residuals from this estimation are used to revise the estimates of ω_{ij}, and the whole procedure is iterated to convergence, it appears that maximum likelihood estimates are obtained.[53] While the two-stage and the iterative procedures are asymptotically equivalent, they obviously produce different estimates for small samples. The choice of an approach, therefore, devolves on the relative small-sample efficiencies of the two techniques. The results of Monte-Carlo studies by Kmenta and Gilbert tend to favour the use (where computer expense does not preclude it) of the iterative technique.[54]

What can be said about the dispersion of these estimators? Except in the highly artificial situation in which $\boldsymbol{X}$ is nonstochastic, the exact variances of the estimates obtained from small samples are unknown. For inference, it is standard procedure to use the asymptotic variance-covariance matrix of $\hat{\boldsymbol{\beta}}$, which may be estimated by[55]

$$\text{est}\ \mathbf{var}\ (\hat{\boldsymbol{\beta}}) = \{(\boldsymbol{X}^*)^T[(\mathbf{\Omega}^*)^{-1} \otimes \boldsymbol{I}_N]\,\boldsymbol{X}^*\}^{-1} \tag{3.106}$$

This allows the normal distribution and the F distribution to be used to conduct approximate significance tests on the values of the estimated parameters,

[52] Zellner, "An Efficient Method of Estimating Seemingly Unrelated Regressions," op. cit.

[53] J. Kmenta and R. F. Gilbert, "Small Sample Properties of Alternative Estimators of Seemingly Unrelated Regressions," *Journal of the American Statistical Association* 63 (December 1968): 1180–1200. Arthur S. Goldberger, "Multivariate Regression: A Descriptive Analysis," Social Systems Research Institute, University of Wisconsin, preliminary draft, November 1969 (mimeo.). Phoebus J. Dhrymes, "Equivalence of Iterative Aitken and Maximum Likelihood Estimators for a System of Regression Equations," *Australian Economic Papers* 10, no. 16 (June 1971): 20–24.

[54] Kmenta and Gilbert, op. cit.

[55] Practices of this sort are strongly criticized in some quarters. See, e.g., R. L. Basmann, "A Note on the Exact Finite Sample Frequency Functions of Generalized Classical Linear Estimators in Two Leading Overidentified Cases," *Journal of the American Statistical Association* 56, no. 295 (September 1961): 619–636.

or to put orders of magnitude on the confidence intervals for parameters.[56] One may test, for instance, to see whether the estimated marginal budget share $\hat{\beta}_i$ of good i differs from its average budget share w_i°; that is, one may test for significant difference from unity of the income elasticities. Or one may test for significant difference from zero of partial substitution elasticities. We explore this more fully in the empirical section below.

3.4.2.3 Empirical Results. Before discussing the empirical results obtained with the model above, it might be as well to put what we are attempting into perspective. In empirical studies of production functions, substitution elasticities between factors of production have proved extremely difficult to estimate.[57] Indeed, the problem has been pathological enough to prompt one worker in the field to write:

> If it was found by Nelson, as quoted by Nerlove, that sizable changes in the elasticity of substitution produce very small effects on the other variables, it should follow that relatively small changes in the other variables should exert strong effects on the elasticity of substitution. The data being what they are, why is it surprising that the magnitude of the elasticity of substitution derived in the several studies jumps all over the place?[58]

As will usually be the case where severe estimation difficulties are encountered, the problem is one of incipient underidentification: many different, competing hypotheses about the substitution elasticities all turn out to be more or less equally satisfactory when matched against the data. The experience in the applied economics of consumption has been no more encouraging than that on the production side. For example, Leser and Powell conducted analyses of postwar consumption patterns in Australia, using virtually identical time series data.[59] Their a priori specifications on the substitution side were radically different—Leser had set all 36 (partial) substitution elasticities in his model to

[56] In the empirical results below Student's t score, rather than the standard normal deviate, has been used to conduct approximate significance tests. There is no theoretical justification for this since the coefficients tend asymptotically to the normal (rather than the Student's) distribution. Insofar as Student's test is somewhat more stringent than the normal test, the procedure can be rationalized as an attempt to make some (albeit slight) allowance for the smallness of the sample size.

[57] See, e.g., Gary P. Sampson, *Productivity Change in Australian Manufacturing*, Ph.D. dissertation, Department of Economics, Monash University, 1969.

[58] Comment by E. Domar on M. Nerlove, "Recent Empirical Studies in the CES and Related Production Functions," in M. Brown, Ed., *The Theory and Empirical Analysis of Production* (New York: Columbia University Press, 1967, for N.B.E.R.), p. 126.

[59] Leser, "Demand Functions for Nine Commodity Groups," op. cit. Alan Powell, "A Complete System of Consumer Demand Equations for the Australian Economy Fitted by a Model of Additive Preferences," *Econometrica* 34, no. 3 (July 1966): 661–675.

Table 3–7

Empirical Comparison of Two Radically Different Substitution Specifications: Postwar Australian Data

Linear Expenditure Equation for Per Capita Consumption of	Coefficient of Multiple Determination R^2			
	Original Expenditure Variables		Transformed Regressands	
	Common Partial Substitution Elasticity = 0.5 (1)	Additive Preferences (0.31, 2.95)[a] (2)	Common Partial Substitution Elasticity = 0.5 (3)	Additive Preferences (0.31, 2.95)[a] (4)
Food	0.998	0.998	0.727	0.742
Clothing	0.990	0.987	0.963	0.950
Housing	0.991	0.991	0.953	0.958
Gas and electricity	0.998	0.997	0.992	0.993
Household durables	0.967	0.968	0.851	0.836
Other goods	0.988	0.989	0.920	0.930
Public transportation	0.986	0.972	0.843	0.767
Tobacco and drink	0.995	0.993	0.820	0.743
Services	0.997	0.996	0.968	0.959
Private transportation	0.995	0.996	0.981	0.986

SOURCE: Alan Powell, "A Complete System of Consumer Demand Equations for the Australian Economy Fitted by a Model of Additive Preferences," *Econometrica* 34, no. 3 (July 1966): 661–675.
Data spanned 1949–50 through 1961–62.
[a] Range of values for estimated different pairwise partial substitution elasticities.

the *same* value; namely, 0.5. In Powell's study, the estimated values of substitution elasticities ranged from 0.31 to 2.95 for different pairs of commodities. Yet measured on any criterion, the "goodness of fit" of the data yielded by the two different approaches was virtually indistinguishable, as can be verified from Table 3–7.[60]

All this has been said by way of introduction to the new empirical estimates published here *because* it turns out that the relatively loose specification based on the triad alone can lead to implausible estimates of partial substitution

[60] Goodness-of-fit statistics are indicative, rather than definitive measures of likely statistical significance of differences between parameter estimates. In those cases in which likelihood ratio tests are available, the relevant contrast is obtained essentially by considering ratios of $(1-R^2)$ for competing hypotheses. This ratio can differ widely from 1, even though both R^2's are "very high."

elasticities. Because of the apparently very low sensitivity of the fit of these models to the specification of substitution effects, more "plausible" values of the substitution elasticities are unlikely to fit the data significantly worse than the "implausible" values actually obtained.[61] Looking at the matter from the viewpoint of our search for quantitative knowledge about the substitutability of various goods in consumption, one is forced to face up to the unpalatable truth: the combined information content of the available data and the postulates of the triad may be insufficient to allow precise inferences about the shape of the "typical" consumer's preference map. But we are running too far ahead.

For numerical simplicity, because of data problems, and also for ease of comparison, a simple four-way split of consumption was used: Food, Clothing, Housing, and Other. Official statistics on consumption at current prices and in real terms were first used to compute the implicit price deflators (which were then used as price indexes). Trends in the series due to general inflation were removed by dividing each expenditure item and each observation on each price index by an index of the general price level. Expenditure figures were expressed on a per capita basis. The data period was 1955 through 1967 in the case of all three countries.

The method of estimation was a simple version of the iterative Aitken-Zellner approach described above. (Thus, only heteroscedasticity between different expenditure equations was taken into account.) Convergence of the estimated marginal value shares to four-digit accuracy or better was reached in five iterations in the case of the United States.[62] The fifth iterates for Canada and Belgium were in some cases accurate to only three digits. In the case of all three countries there was considerable instability in the estimates of the substitution elasticities—at the fifth iterate sometimes not even unit digit convergence had occurred, although generally convergence was better than this. [In the case of the United States, five out of six partial substitution elasticities had reached three-digit accuracy at the fifth iterate, whilst the remaining one (clothing/other) was still *very* unstable.][63] While, in principle, speed of convergence in the computation of estimators and their reliability as measured by their sampling properties are distinct issues, in the present case there was clearly a strong association between the two. A combined R^2 statistic calculated across each set of four equations was output after each iteration. In the case of all three countries, this value exceeded 0.995 after the

---

[61] If some variant of least squares is being used to fit the model, then the sum of squares "valley" has an expansive, relatively flat bottom; if a variant of maximum likelihood, then the likelihood "hill" has a flat top of considerable area.

[62] Convergence to four digits here means four *significant* digits; leading zeros are ignored.

[63] The values for the first five iterations were 0.36981, 0.14508, 0.03268, 0.01208, 0.00868.

first iteration, but showed very little change thereafter. After the fifth iteration the values were: U.S.A., 0.998; Canada, 0.997; Belgium, 0.998. It seemed safe to conclude that any further changes in values of partial substitution elasticities beyond the fifth iteration would lead only to further almost observationally equivalent sets of values for the substitution elasticities. It was therefore decided not to iterate further.

Table 3–8

Summary of Results: Linear Expenditure System Fitted to U.S. Data, 1955–1967, Using Triad Restrictions

Commodity	Estimated Marginal Budget Share $\hat{\beta}_i$	$\|t\|$-Ratio for Previous Column	Estimated Linear Trend Component	$\|t\|$-Ratio for Previous Column
Food	.1172	3.458	−0.0112	0.682
Clothing	.1230	8.756	−0.0147	1.671
Shelter	.0685	2.161	.0505	3.153
Other	.6913	31.220	−0.0247	1.938
Sum	1.0000		0	

Estimated Partial Substitution Elasticities ($|t|$-Ratios in Parentheses)

	Clothing	Shelter	Other
Food	1.120 (1.158)	1.853 (1.204)	−0.394 (1.388)
Clothing		−3.445 (1.307)	0.009 (0.014)
Shelter			2.151 (3.204)

The major results of this empirical work are given in Tables 3–8, 3–9, and 3–10. It will be noted that, for the empirical work, a linear trend term has been added to equation (3.3) before estimation, as a pragmatic gesture towards allowing for changes in tastes. The base year for the trend variable was the middle year of the observation period, 1961.[64] Even after allowing for the difference in classificatory schemes, these results do not agree well with those obtained by Goldberger and Gamaletsos using Stone's LES.[65] These authors used a somewhat different data base; nevertheless, the differences in the estimated marginal value shares are disturbing in the case of the United States

[64] Thus the time index t is set to zero in 1961. The homogeneity of the fitted expenditure system is thus preserved only in this year.

[65] See Arthur S. Goldberger and Theodore Gamaletsos, "A Cross Country Comparison of Consumer Expenditure Patterns," *European Economic Review* 1, no. 3 (Spring 1970): 357–400.

Table 3–9

Summary of Results: Linear Expenditure System Fitted to Canadian Data, 1955–1967, Using Triad Restrictions

Commodity	Estimated Marginal Budget Share $\hat{\beta}_i$	$\|t\|$-Ratio for Previous Column	Estimated Linear Trend Component	$\|t\|$-Ratio for Previous Column
Food	.0891	3.419	2.2654	2.755
Clothing	.0609	5.774	−0.9781	3.154
Shelter	.0401	1.932	5.4591	9.886
Other	.8100	30.779	−6.7464	7.610
Sum	1.0000		0	

Estimated Partial Substitution Elasticities ($|t|$-Ratios in Parentheses)

	Clothing	Shelter	Other
Food	−0.0244 (0.055)	0.9325 (1.733)	0.3316 (2.532)
Clothing		3.6214 (3.665)	−0.1557 (1.141)
Shelter			0.3720 (2.098)

Table 3–10

Summary of Results: Linear Expenditure System Fitted to Belgian Data, 1955–1967, Using Triad Restrictions

Commodity	Estimated Marginal Budget Share $\hat{\beta}_i$	$\|t\|$-Ratio for Previous Column	Estimated Linear Trend Component	$\|t\|$-Ratio for Previous Column
Food	.1683	5.373	.0003	0.680
Clothing	.1069	4.761	.0002	0.533
Shelter	.0361	6.089	−0.0002	2.451
Other	.6886	29.391	−0.0002	0.721
Sum	1.0000		0	

Estimated Partial Substitution Elasticities ($|t|$-Ratios in Parentheses)

	Clothing	Shelter	Other
Food	−0.0646 (0.077)	0.3263 (1.743)	0.9838 (7.388)
Clothing		−3.1353 (2.757)	−0.5851 (0.764)
Shelter			.2427 (1.369)

Table 3–11

Comparison of Estimated Marginal Budget Shares: Stone's LES versus Triad Only

Commodity	Country: Belgium		Canada		U.S.A.	
	Stone	Triad	Stone	Triad	Stone	Triad
Food	.178	.1683	.177	.0891	.081	.1172
Clothing	.098	.1069	.029	.0609	.055	.1230
Shelter	.028	.0361	.279	.0401	.190	.0685
Other	.696	.6886	.515	.8100	.674	.6913

NOTE: Triad assumptions plus linear trend yield homogeneity only at sample mid-point. Systems least-squares results for Stone's LES from Arthur S. Goldberger and Theodore Gamaletsos, "A Cross Country Comparison of Consumer Expenditure Patterns," *European Economic Review* 1, no. 3 (Spring 1970), 357–400.

and Canada. (See Table 3–11.) Only the results for Belgium show fair agreement. The explanation for the wide discrepancies for the United States and Canada lies partially in the inclusion of trends within the LES fitted using triad restrictions.

Be that as it may, six partial substitution elasticities were estimated for each country, a total of eighteen values. Only positive values of cross-substitution elasticities are consistent with well-behaved indifference surfaces. In the estimates tabulated here, seven of the estimated cross-substitution elasticities are negative. (Values of zero have particular interest since they imply that the only demand response of a price change is the income effect.[66]) Although Student's $|t|$ ratio is only the roughest of guides, it does give an indication of the reliability of the estimates. Five of the eighteen estimated values apparently differ significantly from zero at the 5 percent level. They are:

U.S.A.: Shelter/Other, 2.15.
Canada: Food/Other, 0.33; Clothing/Shelter, 3.62.
Belgium: Food/Other, 0.98; Clothing/Shelter, -3.14.

The last of these values has the wrong sign. We are led to conclude that the data do not contain a great deal of useable information on substitution effects. The much stronger prior specification inherent in Stone's LES led, at least in the case of the Australian data discussed above, to a complete set of estimated substitution effects free from errors of sign. Indeed, in a recent multicountry study involving an eight-commodity classification, no sign failures were

[66] Refer to the *fundamental equation of demand theory* (1.62) above. Set $[\kappa_{ij}]$ to zero.

encountered in seventeen out of nineteen countries (the United States being one of the offending cases).[67] The relatively weaker restrictions of the triad, however, may provide a useful inferential framework within which to analyse high-quality bodies of data that are believed, a priori, to contain useful information on substitution. In that case, one might want to avoid the strictures placed on the substitution elasticities by the LES,[68] preferring to estimate average values of these parameters directly in the manner discussed above.

3.4.3 Leser's Approximation

Conrad Leser has estimated a linear expenditure system under the assumption that all pairs of commodities share the same partial substitution elasticity.[69] This amounts to replacing σ_{ij}° in (3.88) above by an unsubscripted constant, σ°. Making this substitution, (3.95) becomes

$$y_{it} = \sigma^{\circ} \sum_{j \neq i} \zeta_{ijt} + \beta_i v_t \tag{3.107}$$

However

$$\begin{aligned}
\sum_{j \neq i} \zeta_{ijt} &= \sum_{j \neq i} \left\{ w_i^{\circ} v_j^{\circ} \left(\frac{p_{jt}}{p_j^{\circ}} - \frac{p_{it}}{p_i^{\circ}} \right) \right\} \\
&= \sum_{j=1}^{k} \left\{ w_i^{\circ} v_j^{\circ} \left(\frac{p_{jt}}{p_j^{\circ}} - \frac{p_{it}}{p_i^{\circ}} \right) \right\} \\
&= \sum_{j=1}^{k} (w_i^{\circ} p_{jt} x_j^{\circ} - w_j^{\circ} p_{it} x_i^{\circ}) \\
&= w_i^{\circ} \sum_{j=1}^{k} p_{jt} x_j^{\circ} - p_{it} x_i^{\circ} = \mathscr{P}_{it} \quad \text{(say)}
\end{aligned} \tag{3.108}$$

Hence the final form of (the systematic part of) Leser's system is

$$y_{it} = \sigma^{\circ} \mathscr{P}_{it} + \beta_i v_t \tag{3.109}$$

Any (additive) error term appended to the RHS of (3.3) would appear without modification on the right of (3.109). Leser has shown how to obtain a systems

---

[67] Lluch and Powell, op. cit.

[68] See the third row of Table 3–1.

[69] Leser, "Demand Functions for Nine Commodity Groups," op. cit.

least-squares fit for (3.109) conditional on a given value of σ°. More general systems methods involve (as before) the deletion of one equation. After this truncation the system may be written

$$\begin{bmatrix} y_1 \\ \\ y_2 \\ \vdots \\ y_{k-1} \end{bmatrix} = \left[\begin{array}{c|cccc} \mathscr{P}_1 & \mathbf{v} & \mathbf{0} & \cdots & \mathbf{0} \\ & & & & \\ \mathscr{P}_2 & \mathbf{0} & \mathbf{v} & \cdots & \mathbf{0} \\ \vdots & \vdots & \vdots & & \\ \mathscr{P}_{k-1} & \mathbf{0} & \mathbf{0} & \cdots & \mathbf{v} \end{array}\right] \begin{bmatrix} \sigma^\circ \\ \beta_1 \\ \beta_2 \\ \vdots \\ \beta_{k-1} \end{bmatrix} + \begin{bmatrix} \boldsymbol{e}_1 \\ \\ \boldsymbol{e}_2 \\ \vdots \\ \boldsymbol{e}_{k-1} \end{bmatrix} \tag{3.110}$$

in which $\boldsymbol{e}_i$ is a vector of N realizations on the stochastic term appended to equation i in (3.3). Aitken and maximum likelihood estimators may be obtained using the procedures discussed above in Section 3.4.2.

3.4.4 Powell's Approximation[70]

If homogeneity and additivity are globally preserved, but other implications of a directly additive utility function are enforced only at certain coordinates, an economy of parameterization is achieved: in particular, the number of price parameters is reduced to one.

In the notation of Chapter 2, λ is the marginal utility of total consumer spending; and in (2.28) ψ is defined as the ratio $\lambda/(\partial\lambda/\partial m)$. Under directly additive preferences we have, from (2.39), that the substitution effects are

$$\kappa_{ij}(t) = -\psi \frac{\partial x_{it}}{\partial m_t} \frac{\partial x_{jt}}{\partial m_t} \tag{3.111}$$

which, in the context of (3.3) becomes,

$$\kappa_{ij}(t) = -\psi \frac{\beta_i \beta_j}{p_{it}\, p_{jt}} \tag{3.112}$$

In these two equations, ψ is (strictly speaking) a variable. We shall denote the value of ψ associated with the coordinate set $(\boldsymbol{p}^\circ; m^\circ)$ by ψ°. Implicitly this constant value will be assumed to be an adequate approximation over the region encompassing the sample data. Using a notation similar to that of

[70] Based on Powell, "A Complete System . . .," op. cit. See also Alan A. Powell, Tran Van Hoa, and R. H. Wilson, "A Multi-Sectoral Analysis of Consumer Demand in the Post-War Period," *Southern Economic Journal* 35, no. 2 (October 1968): 109–120.

(3.77), the fundamental equation of value theory evaluated at $(\boldsymbol{p}^\circ; m^\circ)$ is

$$\frac{\partial x_i^\circ}{\partial p_j^\circ} = -\psi^\circ \frac{\beta_i \beta_j}{p_i^\circ p_j^\circ} - \frac{x_j^\circ \beta_i}{p_i^\circ} \qquad (i \neq j) \tag{3.113}$$

However, within a linear expenditure system (3.3), the LHS of (3.113) is $p_i^\circ a_{ij}$. Hence

$$a_{ij} = -\beta_i \left[\psi^\circ \frac{\beta_j}{p_j^\circ} + x_j^\circ \right] \qquad (i \neq j) \tag{3.114}$$

But global enforcement of the budget constraint—i.e., global "additivity"—implies (3.74b), which gives the diagonal elements a_{ii}:

$$a_{ii} = (1-\beta_i)\left[\psi^\circ \frac{\beta_i}{p_i^\circ} + x_i^\circ \right] \tag{3.115}$$

Substituting from (3.114) and (3.115) into the homogeneous version of (3.3), we obtain (after the addition of stochastic elements e_{it}),

$$y_{it} = \psi^\circ \xi_{it} + \beta_i v_t + e_{it} \tag{3.116}$$

in which v_t and y_{it}, respectively, are as in (3.97) and (3.98); and where

$$\xi_{it} = \beta_i \sum_{j=1}^{k} \beta_j (p_{it}/p_i^\circ - p_{jt}/p_j^\circ) \tag{3.117}$$

The similarity between (3.116) and (3.109) will be immediately evident. However, because ξ_{it} involves cross products in elements of $\boldsymbol{\beta}$, the estimation of (3.116) is very difficult.[71] Although there is no difficulty in writing down the likelihood function of the system, and although the numeric approach to evaluating derivatives (followed by Pollak and Wales) is well developed, at the time of writing only heuristic approaches to the estimation of (3.116) had been implemented.[72]

However, given a $\boldsymbol{\beta}$ vector, the systems least-squares estimation of ψ° in (3.116) is extremely simple; namely

$$\hat{\psi}^\circ = \sum_{t=1}^{N} \sum_{i=1}^{k} Y_{it} \xi_{it} \div \sum_{t=1}^{N} \sum_{i=1}^{k} \xi_{it}^2 \tag{3.118}$$

---

[71] This nonlinearity is much more serious than that of Stone's LES.

[72] Powell, op. cit.; and Powell, Van Hoa, and Wilson, op. cit.

in which

$$Y_{it} \equiv y_{it} - \beta_i v_t \tag{3.119}$$

As a practical matter, (3.118) may be very useful because experience suggests that estimates of the vector $\boldsymbol{\beta}$ are relatively insensitive both to the a priori model specification and to the method of estimation.[73] Consequently, if it is desired to obtain (to a first approximation) estimates of the substitution properties implied by a given set of estimates of marginal budget shares under an additive preference utility specification, then (3.118) is a very convenient vehicle for doing so. Having estimated ψ°, a linear expenditure system for forecasting or other purposes can then easily be recovered using (3.114) and (3.115).

It has been pointed out by Goldberger that the transformation (3.116) of a linear expenditure system "can in fact be obtained *exactly* from maximizing a Stone-Geary utility function provided that the minimum required quantities are known to satisfy a particular pattern."[74] This pattern is[75]

$$\gamma_i = x_i^\circ + \psi_i^\circ \frac{\beta_i}{p_i^\circ} \tag{3.120}$$

Since ψ° is negative, this implies that the minimal quantities γ_i are less than the quantities corresponding to the chosen coordinate set $\{\boldsymbol{p}^\circ; m^\circ\}$ of the exogenous variables. If sample mean prices and total expenditure are chosen for local enforcement of additive preferences, then this interpretation of the transformation (3.116) is plausible (though arbitrary).

---

[73] Lluch and Powell, op. cit., Table 6. In the case of time series data the qualification must be added that models incorporating trends usually give estimated betas differing widely from trend-free models.

[74] Goldberger, "Functional Form and Utility," op. cit., p. 99.

[75] Ibid., p. 99, footnote.

4 Some Rotterdam School Models

The term used for the title of this chapter seems to have been coined by Arthur Goldberger to describe the models developed by Anton Barten and Henri Theil.[1] The first section of the chapter draws very heavily on Theil, Barten, and Goldberger; and on Zaman.[2]

4.1 Demand Equations in Differentials and Differences of Logarithms

4.1.1 Triad Restrictions Only

Consider the total logarithmic differential of the average budget share of good *i*. We have

$$d(\log w_{it}) = d\log(p_{it}x_{it}/m_t)$$

$$= d\log p_{it} + d\log x_{it} - d\log m_t \tag{4.1}$$

Thus

$$dw_{it} = w_i\, d\log p_{it} + w_i\, d\log x_{it} - w_i\, d\log m_t \tag{4.2}$$

From the viewpoint of demand theory, prices $\boldsymbol{p}_t$ ($\equiv [p_{1t}, \ldots, p_{kt}]^T$) and total expenditure m_t are given. Their impact on the quantities is via the demand

[1] Arthur S. Goldberger, "Functional Form and Utility: A Review of Consumer Demand Theory," University of Wisconsin, Systems Formulation, Methodology and Policy Workshop Paper 6703, October 1967. Anton Barten, "Consumer Demand Functions under Conditions of Almost Additive Preferences," *Econometrica* 32, no. 1–2 (January–April 1964): 1–38; "Estimating Demand Equations," *Econometrica* 36, no. 2 (April 1968): 213–251. And Henri Theil, "The Information Approach to Demand Analysis," *Econometrica* 33, no. 1 (January 1965): 67–87; *Economics and Information Theory* (Amsterdam: North-Holland, 1967), pp. 182–275.

[2] Theil, op. cit.; Barten, op. cit.; Goldberger, op. cit.; and Arshad Zaman, *Formulation and Estimation of a Complete System of Demand Equations*, Michigan State University, Econometrics Workshop Special Report No. 3, September 1970, pp. 101–116.

equations (1.2), from which the total quantity differentials may be deduced:

$$dx_{it} = \sum_{j=1}^{k} \frac{\partial x_{it}}{\partial p_{jt}} dp_{jt} + \frac{\partial x_{it}}{\partial m_t} dm_t \tag{4.3}$$

For the *total effects* $(\partial x_{it}/\partial p_{jt})$ we may substitute their partition (1.62) into income effects and specific and general substitution effects, obtaining—after multiplication by (w_{it}/x_{it})—

$$w_i \, d\log x_i = w_i \sum_{j=1}^{k} \left\{ \left[\lambda u^{ij} - \left(\frac{\lambda}{\lambda_m}\right) \frac{\partial x_i}{\partial m} \frac{\partial x_j}{\partial m} - x_j \frac{\partial x_i}{\partial m} \right] \div x_i \right\} dp_j$$

$$+ \, w_i \left(\frac{\partial x_i}{\partial m} \div x_i \right) dm$$

$$= \frac{p_i}{m} \frac{\partial x_i}{\partial m} + \sum_{j=1}^{k} \left[\frac{p_i p_j}{m} \left(\lambda u^{ij} - \psi \frac{\partial x_i}{\partial m} \frac{\partial x_j}{\partial m} - x_j \frac{\partial x_i}{\partial m} \right) \right] d\log p_j \tag{4.4}$$

in which we have simplified the notation by dropping the subscript t; and in which u^{ij} is the (i, j)th element of $\boldsymbol{U}^{-1}$, the inverted Hessian of the utility function; λ is the marginal utility of optimally allocated expenditure; λ_m is the total expenditure derivative of λ; and ψ is (λ/λ_m). *Define* the marginal budget shares by

$$\beta_i = \frac{\partial (p_i x_i)}{\partial m} \tag{4.5}$$

$$= p_i \frac{\partial x_i}{\partial m} \qquad (i = 1, \ldots, k)$$

Then the first term on the right of (4.4) is $\beta_i \, d\log m$. Make the definition

$$v_{ij} = \lambda u^{ij} \frac{p_i p_j}{m} \tag{4.6}$$

and recall the Frisch parameter from (2.41):

$$\omega = \frac{\partial \log \lambda}{\partial \log m} = \frac{m}{\psi} \tag{4.7}$$

Then (4.4) may be written:

$$w_i \, d\log x_i = \beta_i\left(d\log m - \sum_{j=1}^{k} w_i \, d\log p_j\right) + \sum_{j=1}^{k} (v_{ij} - \omega^{-1}\beta_i\beta_j) \, d\log p_j \tag{4.8}$$

The reader will observe the striking similarity between the first right hand term of (4.8) and the corresponding term of (3.5) in the linear expenditure system. However, it is not claimed that a version of (4.8) in which the Greek letters are constant parameters globally represents the behavioral relationship corresponding to any particular utility function; rather (4.8) is meant to give a good local approximation for a variety of utility functions in the region encompassing some data set of interest. Specializations of the utility function result in simplifications of (4.8), as we shall see.

In (4.8), the terms v_{ij} representing specific substitution effects are symmetric. This follows from the symmetry of $\boldsymbol{U}$. A matrix representation of (4.6) is

$$\boldsymbol{N} = [v_{ij}] = (\lambda/m)\hat{\boldsymbol{P}}\boldsymbol{U}^{-1}\hat{\boldsymbol{P}} \tag{4.9}$$

in which $\hat{\boldsymbol{P}}$ is the diagonal matrix having p_i in the ith diagonal position.[3] We continue to hold the assumption that $\boldsymbol{U}$ is negative definite, in which case

$$\sum_{i=1}^{k}\sum_{j=1}^{k} v_{ij} < 0 \tag{4.10}$$

That is,

$$\frac{\lambda}{m}\sum_{i=1}^{k} p_i \sum_{j=1}^{k} u^{ij} p_j < 0 \tag{4.11}$$

But, from (1.58),

$$\sum_{j=1}^{k} u^{ij} p_j = (\lambda_m)^{-1}\frac{\partial x_i}{\partial m} \tag{4.12}$$

Substituting into (4.11) and using (4.7), we have

$$\begin{aligned}\sum_{i=1}^{k}\sum_{j=1}^{k} v_{ij} &= \omega^{-1}\sum_{i=1}^{k} p_i \frac{\partial x_i}{\partial m} \\ &= \omega^{-1}\sum_{i=1}^{k}\beta_i \\ &= \omega^{-1} < 0 \end{aligned} \tag{4.13}$$

[3] If the *time* or *data point* subscript t were to be reintroduced, then there would be N matrices $\hat{\boldsymbol{P}}_t$ with typical diagonal elements p_{it}.

which establishes the negative sign of the Frisch parameter. Notice also that

$$\sum_{j=1}^{k} \nu_{ij} = \omega^{-1}\beta_i \qquad (i = 1, \ldots, k) \tag{4.14}$$

Since ω^{-1} is determined from the elements of N by (4.13), it is natural to eliminate ω in (4.8) before considering estimation. Using (4.14),

$$\omega^{-1}\beta_i\beta_j\, d\log p_j = \sum_{l=1}^{k} \nu_{il}\beta_j\, d\log p_j \tag{4.15}$$

so that, summing over j and then interchanging subscripts l and j,

$$\sum_{j=1}^{k}\left(\sum_{l=1}^{k} \nu_{il}\right)\beta_j\, d\log p_j = \sum_{j=1}^{k} \nu_{ij}\left(\sum_{l=1}^{k} \beta_l\, d\log p_l\right) \tag{4.16}$$

Consequently, (4.8) may be rearranged as

$$\begin{aligned} w_i\, d\log x_i = {} & \beta_i\left[d\log m - \sum_{l=1}^{k} w_l\, d\log p_l\right] \\ & + \sum_{j=1}^{k} \nu_{ij}\left[d\log p_j - \sum_{l=1}^{k} \beta_l\, d\log p_l\right] \end{aligned} \tag{4.17}$$

On the right of this equation, the first term in square brackets gives the logarithmic differential of expenditure deflated by a price index using average budget shares; the second term in square brackets gives a log differential of k relative price variables in which the *marginal* budget shares appear in the weighting scheme.

It is well known that the constant elasticity of demand system (CEDS) violates the additivity requirement $\Sigma p_i x_i = m$ except in the case in which all total expenditure elasticities are unity. The formulation (4.17) suffers from the same difficulty. At the cost of an approximation, however, (4.17) can be altered so as to satisfy additivity. We make use of the approximation

$$d\log m - \sum_{l=1}^{k} w_l\, d\log p_l = \sum_{l=1}^{k} w_l\, d\log x_l \tag{4.18}$$

which is a quadratic approximation in the Taylor series sense.[4]

[4] Theil, *Economics and Information Theory*, op. cit., pp. 222–223.

For empirical work, differentials are replaced by first differences, and w_{it} values by arithmetic averages w_{it}^*:

$$w_{it}^* = \tfrac{1}{2}(w_{it} + w_{i,t-1}) \tag{4.19}$$

If Δ is the backward first-difference operator, and we define the operator D by,

$$\begin{aligned} Dx_t &\equiv \Delta(\log x_t) \\ &\equiv \log x_t - \log x_{t-1} \end{aligned} \tag{4.20}$$

then (4.17) becomes

$$\begin{aligned} w_{it}^* Dx_{it} = {} & \beta_i \left[Dm_t - \sum_{l=1}^{k} w_{lt}^* Dp_{lt} \right] \\ & + \sum_{j=1}^{k} v_{ij} \left[Dp_{jt} - \sum_{l=1}^{k} \beta_l Dp_{lt} \right] \end{aligned} \tag{4.21}$$

Using an approximation analogous to (4.18), (4.21) may be written

$$\begin{aligned} w_{it}^* Dx_{it} = {} & \beta_i \left(\sum_{l=1}^{k} w_{lt}^* Dx_{lt} \right) \\ & + \sum_{j=1}^{k} v_{ij} \left[Dp_{jt} - \sum_{l=1}^{k} \beta_l Dp_{lt} \right] \qquad (i = 1, \ldots, k) \end{aligned} \tag{4.22}$$

in which the first right-hand variable is just the sum over all commodity equations of the left-hand variables. Since by definition the β_i's sum to unity, (4.22) displays the adding-up property provided the sum over i of the second right-hand term of (4.22) vanishes. But

$$\begin{aligned} \sum_{i=1}^{k} \sum_{j=1}^{k} v_{ij} \left[Dp_{jt} - \sum_{l=1}^{k} \beta_l Dp_{lt} \right] &= \sum_{j=1}^{k} Dp_{jt} \sum_{i=1}^{k} v_{ij} \\ &\quad - \left(\sum_{j=1}^{k} \sum_{i=1}^{k} v_{ij} \right) \sum_{l=1}^{k} \beta_l Dp_{lt} \\ &= \sum_{j=1}^{k} Dp_{jt} \cdot \omega^{-1} \beta_j - \omega^{-1} \sum_{l=1}^{k} \beta_l Dp_{lt} \qquad (4.23) \\ &= 0 \end{aligned}$$

where we have used (4.14) in conjunction with the symmetry of v_{ij}, and (4.13). [Notice that this additivity requirement would be lost without the approximation (4.18).] Equation (4.23) and its particularizations are the basis of the later Rotterdam School work. Note that in (4.22) no specialization of the utility function beyond negative definiteness of the Hessian has been made—fitting (4.22) is, therefore, closely analogous to fitting the *triad-only* version of the LES discussed above.

Of course, before (4.22) can be fitted, it is necessary to decide which terms are variables and which parameters. In general—that is, for an arbitrary classical utility function—we would expect marginal budget shares β_i to be variable, and also the substitution-based elements v_{ij}. It is the Rotterdam tradition to assume the β_i are constants (linear Engel curves), and that the v_{ij}, or some function of them such as ω, are constant.

The final form, (4.22), is nonlinear in its parameters and fitting (whether by systems least squares, Aitken methods, or maximum likelihood) involves iterative search procedures such as those mentioned above in Chapter 3. By contrast, the *triad-only* transform (3.99) of the LES is relatively uncomplicated to estimate. Equation (4.22), on the other hand, by working in logs of first differences, goes a long way towards eliminating heteroscedasticity and autocorrelation which frequently beset fitted versions of linear expenditure systems.[5]

4.1.2 *Additive-Preference Version*

Under directly additive preferences, $\boldsymbol{U}$ and $\boldsymbol{U}^{-1}$ are diagonal, so that in (4.6), v_{ij} vanishes for all i different from j. Consequently, (4.22) may be rewritten

$$w_{it}^{*}\, Dx_{it} = \beta_i\left(\sum_{l=1}^{k} w_{lt}^{*}\, Dx_{lt}\right) + \omega^{-1}\beta_i \sum_{j=1}^{k}\left[Dp_{jt} - \sum_{l=1}^{k} \beta_l\, Dp_{lt}\right] \tag{4.24}$$

in which,

$$\omega^{-1}\beta_i = v_{ii} \tag{4.25}$$

which may be seen in the light of (4.14) from the fact that $\Sigma_j v_{ij} \equiv v_{ii}$ under additive preferences. The analogue of (4.24) in the case of the LES is Powell's approximation, (3.116). The nonlinearities in (4.24) are of the same order of difficulty as those in (3.116).

The estimation of (4.24) or (4.22) of course, depends on the error specification. The pragmatic approach would involve appending additive zero mean errors to the nonstochastic final forms. The preservation of the adding-up

[5] Of course, (3.99) could also be fitted in first differences.

property once again leads to singularity in the variance-covariance matrix; the solution, as before, involves arbitrary deletion of one equation.[6] However, in his 1968 paper, Barten eschews the arbitrary appending of errors onto final forms, preferring to incorporate the stochastic influence directly into the utility function.[7] This is done at the cost of assuming (i) that the underlying utility function can be approximated over the relevant range of variation by a quadratic function; and (ii) that the random influences enter this utility function through the additive term only. The approach is elegant, but complicates estimation.[8]

4.2 Partitioning Price Elasticities

4.2.1 General and Specific Substitution Effects

Following Barten, we may use the expressions (2.50) and (1.62) to separate out three conceptually distinct elements of price elasticity.[9] Under classical conditions, the fundamental equations of demand theory are

$$\boldsymbol{X}_p = -\boldsymbol{x}_m \boldsymbol{x}^T + \lambda \boldsymbol{U}^{-1} - \psi \boldsymbol{x}_m \boldsymbol{x}_m^T \tag{4.26a}$$

Under almost additive preferences this becomes

$$\boldsymbol{X}_p = -\boldsymbol{x}_m \boldsymbol{x}^T - [\lambda \hat{\boldsymbol{U}}^{-1} (\boldsymbol{I} - \boldsymbol{H}) \hat{\boldsymbol{U}}^{-1} + \psi \boldsymbol{x}_m \boldsymbol{x}_m^T] \tag{4.26b}$$

where (it will be recalled) $\boldsymbol{x}_m$ is the $k \times 1$ vector with elements $(\partial x_i/\partial m)$; $\boldsymbol{X}_p$ is the $k \times k$ matrix with elements $[\partial x_i/\partial p_j]$; $\boldsymbol{U}$ is the Hessian of the utility function, u; $\hat{\boldsymbol{U}}$ is the diagonal matrix with typical element $(\sqrt{-u_{ii}})$, where $u_{ii} \equiv \partial^2 u/\partial x_i^2$. And where $\boldsymbol{H}$ is a matrix which contains zeros for entries corresponding to pairs from different preference blocks, which has zeros on the principal diagonal, and which has nonzero elements taking the form

$$h_{ij} = -u_{ij}(u_{ii} u_{jj})^{-1/2} \tag{4.27}$$

---

[6] Anton Barten, "Maximum Likelihood Estimation of a Complete System of Consumer Demand Equations," *European Economic Review* 1, no. 1 (Fall 1969): 7–73.

[7] Barten, "Estimating Demand Equations," op. cit.

[8] For a textbook treatment of Barten's development of the system under a stochastic utility function, see J. L. Bridge, *Applied Econometrics* (Amsterdam: North-Holland, 1971), pp. 116–128.

[9] This section follows Barten, "Consumer Demand Functions . . .," op. cit., pp. 3–7.

where, from the definition of almost additivity, the h_{ij} are less than one in absolute value.

To understand the distinction made between the general substitution effect $\psi \boldsymbol{x}_m \boldsymbol{x}^T$, and the specific substitution effect $\lambda \boldsymbol{U}^{-1}$, it is helpful to remember that directly additive preferences involve *no interactions at all* between commodities—the utility Hessian is a diagonal matrix. Interactions between commodities show up in the off-diagonal positions of the Hessian. When $\boldsymbol{U}$ is diagonal, so is $\lambda \boldsymbol{U}^{-1}$, and cross-substitution effects κ_{ij} $(i \neq j)$ reduce as we have seen to just $\psi \boldsymbol{x}_m \boldsymbol{x}^T$. When $\boldsymbol{U}$ is nondiagonal, the appropriate element of $\lambda \boldsymbol{U}^{-1}$ must be added to $\psi \boldsymbol{x}_m \boldsymbol{x}^T$ to obtain the substitution effect. Since the term $\lambda \boldsymbol{U}^{-1}$ arises only through interaction between commodities, it has been termed the "specific" substitution effect; $\psi \boldsymbol{x}_m \boldsymbol{x}^T$, on the other hand, has been called the "general" substitution effect.[10]

These three elements of price elasticity—income effect, general and specific substitution effects—may be expressed in terms of elasticities.

To convert the uncompensated derivatives $\boldsymbol{X}_p$ into elasticities, the following two diagonal matrices are useful:

$$\hat{\boldsymbol{X}} = \begin{bmatrix} x_1 & 0 & 0 & \cdots & 0 \\ 0 & x_2 & 0 & \cdots & 0 \\ \vdots & & & & \\ 0 & 0 & 0 & \cdots & x_k \end{bmatrix} \tag{4.28}$$

$$\hat{\boldsymbol{P}} = \begin{bmatrix} p_1 & 0 & 0 & \cdots & 0 \\ 0 & p_2 & 0 & \cdots & 0 \\ \vdots & & & & \\ 0 & 0 & 0 & \cdots & p_k \end{bmatrix} \tag{4.29}$$

Then the matrix of (ordinary) price elasticities is

$$\boldsymbol{G} = \underset{k \times k}{[\eta_{ij}]} = \left[\frac{p_j}{x_i}\frac{\partial x_i}{\partial p_j}\right] = \hat{\boldsymbol{X}}^{-1}\boldsymbol{X}_p\hat{\boldsymbol{P}} \tag{4.30}$$

Similarly, the vector of income elasticities is

$$\boldsymbol{E} = [E_i] = m\hat{\boldsymbol{X}}^{-1}\boldsymbol{x}_m \tag{4.31}$$

[10] The latter terminology is risky, since there is danger of confusing "general" with "all-embracing": we are, in fact, referring only to part of the substitution effect in the general case. The terminology, nevertheless, is standard.

If we premultiply (4.26a and b) by $\hat{X}^{-1}$ and post-multiply by $\hat{P}$, we obtain

$$G = G_1 + G_2 + G_3 \tag{4.32}$$

where

$$G_1 = [\eta_{1ij}] = -\hat{X}^{-1}x_m x^T\hat{P} \tag{4.33a}$$

is the matrix whose elements are components of price elasticity due to the income effect. The second term of the RHS of (4.32) is the matrix

$$G_2 = [\eta_{2ij}] = \lambda\hat{X}^{-1}U^{-1}\hat{P}$$

Under almost additive preferences this becomes (4.33b)

$$G_2 = -\lambda\hat{X}^{-1}\hat{U}^{-1}(I-H)\hat{U}^{-1}\hat{P}$$

These matrices have, as elements, components of price elasticity due to specific substitution effects. Finally, in the matrix

$$G_3 = [\eta_{3ij}] = -\psi\hat{X}^{-1}x_m x_m^T\hat{P} \tag{4.33c}$$

are arrayed the components of price elasticity due to the general substitution effect.

4.2.2 Specific Substitution Effect Related to Income Elasticities and to Homogeneity of Demand

We have for some time been focussed on price derivatives of consumption. These, however, constitute only one term of the solution of the fundamental matrix equation of value theory. The other term is the vector of income derivatives displayed in equation (1.58). First, substituting from (1.58) into the expression (4.31) above for the income elasticities, we obtain

$$E = \lambda_m m\hat{X}^{-1}U^{-1}p \tag{4.34}$$

and, from (2.42),

$$E = \omega\hat{X}^{-1}(\lambda U^{-1}p)$$

This expression is reminiscent of the definition (4.33b) of the elasticities G_2 reflecting specific interactions. In order to relate the two we first observe that the effect of summing the rows of the diagonal matrix $\hat{P}$ is just to produce once again the price vector p from which $\hat{P}$ was constructed; that is

$$\underset{k\times k}{\hat{P}}\ \underset{k\times 1}{1} = \underset{k\times 1}{p} \tag{4.35}$$

in which $\mathbf{1}$ is a column vector of k units (the "summation vector"). Proceeding, we post-multiply (4.33b) by $\mathbf{1}$, obtaining

$$\begin{aligned} \boldsymbol{G}_2\mathbf{1} &= \lambda\hat{\boldsymbol{X}}^{-1}\boldsymbol{U}^{-1}\hat{\boldsymbol{P}}\mathbf{1} \\ &= \hat{\boldsymbol{X}}^{-1}(\lambda\boldsymbol{U}^{-1}\boldsymbol{p}) \\ &= \frac{1}{\omega}\boldsymbol{E} \qquad \text{[from (4.34)]} \end{aligned} \tag{4.36}$$

This is a set of k constraints relating income elasticities to specific substitution effects—it states that the sum of the k components of price elasticity of good i due to its specific interactions with other goods (and with itself) is equal to its income elasticity divided by the income elasticity of the marginal utility of income.[11]

4.2.3 Symmetry Restriction on Elasticities

We need to take account of the fact that the matrix $\boldsymbol{U}^{-1}$ within the product $\boldsymbol{G}_2$ in (4.33b) is symmetric.[12] In Chapter 1, elasticities ε_{ij} were defined [in (1.47)] as income-compensated cross elasticities of consumption of goods i with respect to prices j ($i, j = 1, \ldots, k$; $i \neq j$). Hence

$$\varepsilon_{ij} = \eta_{2ij} + \eta_{3ij} \qquad (i \neq j) \tag{4.37}$$

that is, these ε-elasticities are merely the sum of the components of price elasticity due to the specific and the general substitution effects. We also recall from Chapter 1 that the ε-elasticities are equal to the corresponding substitution elasticities $\{\sigma_{ij}\}$, weighted by the appropriate budget shares; that is,

$$\varepsilon_{ij}/w_j = \sigma_{ij} \tag{4.38}$$

The symmetry of the substitution elasticities σ_{ij} implies

$$w_i\varepsilon_{ij} = w_j\varepsilon_{ji} \tag{4.39}$$

---

[11] The result (4.36) can also be viewed as the consequence of the *homogeneity* of the demand function. From Chapter 1 we recall that a commodity's own- and cross-price elasticities add to the negative of its income elasticity—equation (1.5c). Using this result in conjunction with two other results below one arrives at (4.36) by an alternative route.

[12] The *entire* substitution term is, of course, symmetric. In its other component, $\boldsymbol{G}_3$, symmetry is automatically preserved if estimation proceeds via the income effects $\boldsymbol{x}_m$. This means that only the term $\boldsymbol{G}_2$ need explicitly be constrained to symmetry.

Apply (4.39) to (4.37):

$$w_i\eta_{2ij} + w_i\eta_{3ij} = w_j\eta_{2ji} + w_j\eta_{3ji} \qquad (i, j=1, \ldots, k;\ i\neq j) \qquad (4.40)$$

The η_3 parts of this equation are equal on both sides; for

$$\begin{aligned}\eta_{3ij}w_i &= -\psi\frac{p_j}{x_i}\frac{\partial x_i}{\partial m}\frac{\partial x_j}{\partial m}\cdot\frac{p_i x_i}{m}\\ &= -\psi\frac{p_i}{x_j}\frac{\partial x_i}{\partial m}\frac{\partial x_j}{\partial m}\cdot\frac{p_i x_i}{m}\cdot\frac{p_j}{p_i}\cdot\frac{x_j}{x_i} \qquad (4.41)\\ &= \eta_{3ji}w_j\end{aligned}$$

As a result, equivalently to (4.40) we may write

$$w_i\eta_{2ij} = w_j\eta_{2ji} \qquad (i, j=1, \ldots, k;\ i\neq j) \qquad (4.42)$$

Using $\hat{W}$ as the diagonal matrix whose nonzero elements are the k budget shares, (4.42) becomes in matrix notation

$$\underset{k\times k}{\hat{W}}\ \underset{k\times k}{G_2} = \underset{k\times k}{G_2^T}\ \underset{k\times k}{\hat{W}} \qquad (4.43)$$

4.2.4 Additivity Constraint on Elasticities

The full list of constraints on the elasticities can now be spelled out. Although a large number of equivalent formulations are possible, here we follow Barten.[13] Once again we hark back to budget *additivity* as the starting point.

$$\sum_{i=1}^{k} v_i \equiv \sum_{i=1}^{k} p_i x_i \equiv m$$

Differentiating partially with respect to m, we obtain

$$\sum_{i=1}^{k} w_i E_i = 1 \qquad (4.44)$$

[13] "Estimating Demand Equations . . .," op. cit.

4.2.5 *General Substitution Effects Related to Income Elasticities*

The matrix G_3 of price elasticity components has k^2 elements; these are generated, however, by the k income derivatives plus one additional parameter (ψ). Working in elasticity terms, we write a typical element of (4.33c) as

$$\eta_{3ij} = -\psi \frac{p_j}{x_i} \frac{\partial x_i}{\partial m} \frac{\partial x_j}{\partial m}$$

$$= -\frac{\psi}{m} \cdot \frac{m}{x_i} \cdot \frac{\partial x_i}{\partial m} \cdot \frac{m}{x_j} \frac{\partial x_j}{\partial m} \frac{p_j x_j}{m}$$

$$= -\omega^{-1} E_i E_j w_j \qquad (i, j = 1, \ldots, k) \tag{4.45}$$

4.2.6 *Income Effects Related to Income Elasticities*

The final constraint is the most straightforward of all. From (4.33a)

$$\eta_{1ij} = -\frac{p_j}{x_i} \frac{\partial x_i}{\partial m} \cdot x_j$$

$$= -\frac{\partial x_i}{\partial m} \cdot \frac{m}{x_i} \cdot \frac{p_j x_j}{m}$$

$$= -w_j E_i \qquad (i, j = 1, \ldots, k) \tag{4.46}$$

4.3 Constant Elasticity Demand System

It was pointed out above that (4.22) could be regarded as a triad-based transform of a constant elasticity of demand system (CEDS). The CEDS may be written

$$\log_e x_{it} = \sum_{j=1}^{k} \eta_{ij} \log_e p_{jt} + E_i \log_e m_t + c_i t \tag{4.47}$$

where any autonomous trends in consumption have been regarded as exponential, $100c_i$ being the percentage autonomous growth in the demand for i per unit time period. If errors are appended additively to (4.47), and these are strongly positively autocorrelated, one would prefer to work with the first differences of (4.47):

$$Dx_{it} = \sum_{j=1}^{k} \eta_{ij}\, Dp_{jt} + E_i\, Dm_t + c_i \qquad (4.48)$$

(The operator D takes backward first differences of logarithms, as before.)[14] Substituting the decomposition (4.32) for η_{ij} into (4.48) and using (4.45) and (4.46), equation (4.48) becomes

$$Dx_{it} = \sum_{j=1}^{k} (-w_j E_i + \eta_{2ij} - \omega^{-1} E_i E_j w_j)\, Dp_{jt} + E_i\, Dm_t + c_i \qquad (4.49)$$

$$= c_i + \sum_{j=1}^{k} \eta_{2ij}\, Dp_{jt} + E_i \left\{ Dm_t - \sum_{j=1}^{k} w_j (1 + \omega^{-1} E_j)\, Dp_{jt} \right\}$$

The empirical problem is to fit (4.49) subject to the constraints (4.36), (4.43), and (4.44). After specializing the utility function, Barten explores a set of linearizations and iterative procedures to cope with the extreme nonlinearities of the specification and the complexity of the constraints. Additional complications taken into account are prior stochastic information on own price elasticities and nonstochastic information on the relative magnitudes of variances.[15] Here we shall consider only a highly simplified scheme for the estimation of (4.49).

4.3.1 Constrained Aitken Estimator[16]

Perhaps the easiest format in which to approach the estimation problem is the "stacked regression" method used by Zellner.[17] The advantage of this format is that restrictions that involve parameters from *different* commodity equations involve only parameters from the same "super" regression equation in the

---

[14] Equation (4.48) is the form adopted by Barten in "Consumer Demand Functions . . .," op. cit.

[15] "Consumer Demand Functions . . .," op. cit.

[16] The development in this section is in the spirit of the treatments by Robin Court "Utility Maximization and the Demand for New Zealand Meats," *Econometrica* 35, no. 3–4 (July–October 1967): 424–446; and Ray Byron "Methods for Estimating Demand Equations Using Prior Information," *Australian Economic Papers* 7, no. 11 (December 1968): 227–248.

[17] Arnold Zellner, "An Efficient Method of Estimating Seemingly Unrelated Regressions and Tests for Aggregation Bias," *Journal of the American Statistical Association* 57, no. 298 (June 1962): 348–368.

new format. The approach is conveniently illustrated by the two commodity case ($k = 2$). In this case (4.49) becomes

$$Dx_{1t} = \eta_{11}\, Dp_{1t} + \eta_{12}\, Dp_{2t} + E_1\, Dm_t + c_1\, t + e_{1t} \qquad (4.50a)$$

$$Dx_{2t} = \eta_{21}\, Dp_{2t} + \eta_{22}\, Dp_{2t} + E_2\, Dm_t + c_2\, t + e_{2t} \qquad (4.50b)$$

where

$$\eta_{ij} = (\eta_{2ij} - w_j\, E_i - \omega^{-1} w_j\, E_i\, E_j) \qquad (4.50c)$$

and where e_{1t} and e_{2t} are zero mean random errors which have been appended to (4.48). The stacked regression is

$$\begin{bmatrix} \mathbf{x}_1^* \\ \mathbf{x}_2^* \end{bmatrix} = \begin{bmatrix} \mathbf{p}_1^* & \mathbf{p}_2^* & \mathbf{m}^* & \mathbf{t} & \mathbf{0} & \mathbf{0} & \mathbf{0} & \mathbf{0} \\ \mathbf{0} & \mathbf{0} & \mathbf{0} & \mathbf{0} & \mathbf{p}_1^* & \mathbf{p}_2^* & \mathbf{m}^* & \mathbf{t} \end{bmatrix} \begin{bmatrix} \eta_{11} \\ \eta_{12} \\ E_1 \\ c_1 \\ \eta_{21} \\ \eta_{22} \\ E_2 \\ c_2 \end{bmatrix} + \begin{bmatrix} \mathbf{e}_1 \\ \mathbf{e}_2 \end{bmatrix} \qquad (4.51)$$

where the starred entities are $N \times 1$ observation vectors on the differences of the logarithms of the corresponding unstarred variables, and $\mathbf{t}$ is the vector $(1, 2, \ldots, N)^T$. Since only exogenous variables appear on the right of (4.50a and b), ordinary least squares residuals can be used to obtain a consistent estimate of the contemporaneous variance-covariance matrix for the errors; that is, a consistent estimate of

$$\mathbf{\Omega} = E\left[\begin{array}{c|c} e_1^2\, \mathbf{I}_N & e_1 e_2\, \mathbf{I}_N \\ \hline e_1 e_2\, \mathbf{I}_N & e_2^2\, \mathbf{I}_N \end{array}\right] \qquad (4.52)$$

can be obtained.[18] The Aitken estimator of (4.52) then yields consistent estimates of the η_{ij}'s and of E_1, E_2, c_1, and c_2. Rather than compute the ordinary Aitken estimator, however, one can build in the consequences of

[18] Equation (4.52) has been written on the assumption that own- and cross-serial covariances vanish, but allows for possibly nonvanishing contemporaneous covariances. The lack of global additivity of the constant elasticity of demand system avoids the singularity problem encountered elsewhere with variance-covariance matrices.

additivity, *homogeneity*, and *symmetry* at this stage of the estimation. In particular, our estimates should satisfy

HOMOGENEITY REQUIREMENT

$$\sum_{j=1}^{k} \eta_{ij} = -E_i \qquad (i = 1, \ldots, k) \tag{4.53}$$

as well as

ADDITIVITY REQUIREMENT

$$\sum_{i=1}^{k} w_i^\circ E_i = 1 \tag{4.54}$$

in which $\{w^\circ\}$ is a set of budget shares at which additivity is to hold (since in this constant-elasticity system it cannot hold globally).

From (4.50c) it can be seen that, equivalent to the symmetry constraint (4.42), i.e., that $w_i^\circ \eta_{2ij} = w_j^\circ \eta_{2ji}$, is the requirement that

SYMMETRY REQUIREMENT

$$w_i^\circ \eta_{ij} + w_i^\circ w_j^\circ E_i = w_j^\circ \eta_{ji} + w_j^\circ w_i^\circ E_j \qquad (\text{all } i \neq j) \tag{4.55}$$

Suppose we denote by $\boldsymbol{\Theta}$ the 8×1 parameter vector on the RHS of (4.51). Making use of the constraints of (4.53), (4.54), and (4.55), our aim is to estimate $\boldsymbol{\Theta}$ in (4.51) subject to

$$[\,0 \quad 0 \quad w_1^\circ \quad 0, \quad 0 \quad 0 \quad w_2^\circ \quad 0\,]\,\boldsymbol{\Theta} = 1 \qquad [\text{from (4.54)}] \quad (4.56\text{a})$$

$$\begin{bmatrix} 1 & 1 & 1 & 0, & 0 & 0 & 0 & 0 \\ 0 & 0 & 0 & 0, & 1 & 1 & 1 & 0 \end{bmatrix} \boldsymbol{\Theta} = \begin{bmatrix} 0 \\ 0 \end{bmatrix} \qquad [\text{from (4.53)}] \quad (4.56\text{b})$$

and

$$[0, w_1^\circ, (w_1^\circ w_2^\circ), 0; -w_2^\circ, 0, (-w_1^\circ w_2^\circ), 0]\,\boldsymbol{\Theta} = 0 \qquad [\text{from (4.55)}] \quad (4.56\text{c})$$

If we denote by $\boldsymbol{R}$ the 4×8 matrix[19] whose rows are displayed in (4.56a, b, c), then this set of *triad*-based constraints may be written as

$$\boldsymbol{R\Theta} = \boldsymbol{r} \tag{4.57}$$

[19] In general the dimensions of $\boldsymbol{R}$ will be $\{1 + k + \frac{1}{2}k(k-1)\} \times [2k + k^2]$; i.e., $[1 + \frac{1}{2}k(k+1)] \times [k(k+2)]$.

where

$$r = (1 \ 0 \ 0 \ 0)^T \tag{4.58}$$

The rank of $\boldsymbol{R}$, it will be noted, is full. The solution of this estimation problem is almost standard;[20] a brief sketch is all that is required here. Given the lack of global additivity of the CEDS, the rank of $\boldsymbol{\Omega}$ in (4.52) will be full. In that case there exists a nonsingular matrix $\boldsymbol{F}$ such that[21]

$$\boldsymbol{F}^T\boldsymbol{F} = \boldsymbol{\Omega}^{-1} \tag{4.59}$$

(It is true, of course, that $\boldsymbol{F}$ will not be known; it can, however, be estimated consistently in a variety of ways, including a first-round ordinary least squares estimation of the e's which are then used to estimate $\boldsymbol{\Omega}$ and subsequently $\boldsymbol{F}$. In what follows, we will write $\boldsymbol{F}$, but mean it to be replaced by a consistent estimate in operational applications.)

Premultiplication of (4.51) by $(\boldsymbol{F} \otimes \boldsymbol{I})$ gives a system with a classical error structure (or one which converges in probability to such a system). The transformed system involves the same slope vector $\boldsymbol{\Theta}$ as (4.51). The theory of fitting a classical system subject to nonstochastic constraints of the form (4.57) is well known.[22]

If the matrix on the right of (4.51) after premultiplication by $(\boldsymbol{F} \otimes \boldsymbol{I})$ is $\boldsymbol{Z}^*$, then the constrained Aitken estimator is[23]

$$\begin{aligned}\hat{\boldsymbol{\Theta}} = {} & [(\boldsymbol{Z}^*)^T\boldsymbol{Z}^*]^{-1}(\boldsymbol{Z}^*)^T\boldsymbol{y}^* + [(\boldsymbol{Z}^*)^T\boldsymbol{Z}^*]^{-1}\boldsymbol{R}^T\{\boldsymbol{R}[(\boldsymbol{Z}^*)^T\boldsymbol{Z}^*]^{-1}\boldsymbol{R}^T\}^{-1} \\ & \times \{\boldsymbol{r} - \boldsymbol{R}[(\boldsymbol{Z}^*)^T\boldsymbol{Z}^*]^{-1}(\boldsymbol{Z}^*)^T\boldsymbol{y}^*\}\end{aligned} \tag{4.60}$$

in which $\boldsymbol{y}^*$ is the left-hand vector of (4.51) after premultiplication by $(\boldsymbol{F} \otimes \boldsymbol{I})$. At this point we will have fitted a *triad*-based transform of the CEDS. All of the $[k+1+\frac{1}{2}k(k-1)]$ constraints reflecting homogeneity (4.53), additivity (4.54), and symmetry (4.55) will be fully reflected in the estimates. Consequently, the specific substitution effects and Frisch parameter in (4.50c) are not identified, since to solve for them from a knowledge of the η_{ij}'s, E_i's and w_i°'s would involve $[\frac{1}{2}k(k-1)]$ linearly independent equations in $[\frac{1}{2}k(k-1)+1]$ unknowns. The specific substitution effects do become identified, however, if an extraneous estimate of the Frisch parameter ω is available. And of course, additional information on the utility function could serve to identify ω, as we shall see below.

---

[20] A. S. Goldberger, *Econometric Theory* (New York: Wiley, 1964), pp. 255–258.

[21] Ibid., p. 234.

[22] Ibid.

[23] Ibid., p. 257.

4.3.2 *Additive-Preference Version*

Under additive preferences, the Hessian $\boldsymbol{U}$ of the utility function is diagonal. Hence, from (4.33b), we have

$$\eta_{2ij} = \frac{\lambda p_i}{x_i u_{ii}} \tag{4.61a}$$

$$\eta_{2ij} = 0 \qquad (\text{for all } i \neq j) \tag{4.61b}$$

But from (2.19) the principal diagonal elements of $\boldsymbol{U}$ are

$$u_{ii}[\equiv \phi_i''] = \frac{p_i \lambda_m}{\partial x_i / \partial m} \tag{4.62}$$

Hence,

$$\eta_{2ii} = \omega^{-1} E_i \tag{4.63}$$

Substituting from (4.63) and (4.61b) into (4.50c) gives us for $i \neq j$

$$\eta_{ij} = -E_i w_j^\circ (1 + \omega^{-1} E_j) \tag{4.64a}$$

and for $i = j$

$$\eta_{ii} = E_i [\omega^{-1} - w_i^\circ (1 + \omega^{-1} E_i)] \tag{4.64b}$$

Within this additive-preference framework the homogeneity requirement (4.53) and the symmetry requirement (4.55) are *automatically* preserved provided the additivity requirement (4.54) is met. The problem, then, is to estimate (4.48) subject to (4.64a) and (4.64b). Unlike the *triad* version discussed in the last section, the constraints among the elasticities do not have a linear representation. As with the corresponding transformation (3.116) of a linear expenditure system, iterative fitting procedures are required.

It will be noted that in the present system the elasticity with respect to total expenditure of the marginal utility of expenditure (i.e., Frisch's ω) is taken as constant; in Stone's LES, on the other hand, it is a critical variable—see equation (3.16). In Powell's approximate treatment of the LES, the ratio $[\lambda/(\partial\lambda/\partial m)]$ is constant, so that $|\omega|$ is proportional to m_t (which is a counter-intuitive result).

4.3.3 *Version Based on Almost Additive, Block-Independent Preferences*

Almost additive preferences provides a simplification as compared with the general case; it does not lead directly, as we have seen, to any shrinkage of the parameter space. To reiterate, the reason is that the matrix $\boldsymbol{H}$ of equation (2.45) potentially has as many distinct, nonzero, values, as there are specific substitution effects. However, by specifying independence between certain pairs of commodities, the number of parameters may be reduced. Here, by "independence" is meant the following: commodities i and j are independent if the marginal utility of i is not a function of the consumption of j, and *vice versa.*[24] Commodities that are not independent are said to "interact." In the case of block-independent preferences, the utility function cannot be written as a sum of k partial functions—as in (2.16), which defines directly additive preferences. The utility function can, however, be written as a sum of fewer than k partial utility functions, with at least one of these partial utility functions having the consumption of two or more commodities as arguments. The commodities included within a particular partial utility function are said to constitute a *preference block*. If there are n blocks, and $v(l)$ $(l = 1, \ldots, n)$, is the number of arguments of the lth block, the block-independent utility function is written as[25]

$$\Phi = \Phi_1(x_1, x_2, \ldots, x_{v(1)}) + \Phi_2(x_{v(1)+1}, \ldots, x_{v(1)+v(2)}) + \cdots$$
$$+ \Phi_n(x_{v(1)+v(2)+\cdots+v(n-1)+1}, \ldots, x_k) \qquad \left[\sum_{l=1}^{n} v(l) = k\right] \tag{4.65}$$

In (4.65) it is clear that the marginal utility of any good (good number j, say) within block r is the partial derivative of Φ_r with respect to x_j. Call this derivative $\Phi_r'(j)$. This new function has exactly the same arguments as Φ_r. Consequently, all of the derivatives of $\Phi_r'(j)$ with respect to x's outside of block r are zero. On the other hand, *some* of the derivatives of $\Phi_r'(j)$ with respect to x's inside block r *may* be zero. More formally, we shall define a subset r of commodities as a preference block if it satisfies the following rules:[26]

$$u_{ij} = \frac{\partial^2 \Phi}{\partial x_i \, \partial x_j} = 0 \qquad \begin{cases} \text{for all pairs of commodities} \\ i, j, \text{ such that } i \in r, j \notin r. \end{cases} \tag{4.66a}$$

$$u_{ij} = \frac{\partial^2 \Phi}{\partial x_i \, \partial x_j} \neq 0 \qquad \begin{cases} \text{There is at least one value of} \\ j \in r \ (j \neq i) \text{ which makes this} \\ \text{statement true for each and} \\ \text{every } i \in r. \end{cases} \tag{4.66b}$$

---

[24] In view of the Goldman-Uzawa theorem (2.2), this definition is consistent with that given above in (2.1) for any scheme involving more than two preference blocks.

[25] See equation (2.4).

[26] Blocks containing only one element obviously must be exempted from the second requirement.

Blocks are constructed, therefore, in such a way that any commodity within a block interacts with at least one other commodity within the block, whilst no two commodities drawn from different blocks interact.

The block diagonal form (2.5) of the Hessian of Φ immediately implies that certain elements of $\boldsymbol{H}$ in the definition (2.45) of almost additive preferences are "known" a priori to be zero. In Barten's seminal paper in which he combines block-independence with almost additive preferences, a fourteen-commodity split was used.[27] No single commodity was assumed to interact with more than three other commodities; more commonly, commodities were assumed to interact with only one or two other commodities. Barten's prior ideas on these interactions are reproduced in Table 4–1.

Table 4–1

Barten's Specification of Interactions Among 14 Commodity Groups

Commodity Group	Interactions with
(1) Groceries	2, 3, 4
(2) Dairy products	1, 4, 5
(3) Vegetables & fruit	1
(4) Meat & meat products	1, 2, 5
(5) Fish	2, 4
(6) Confectionery, chocolate, ice cream	7, 8
(7) Tobacco products	6, 8
(8) Drinks	6, 7
(9) Bread	nil
(10) Textiles & clothing	11
(11) Footwear	10
(12) Household articles & furniture	13
(13) Other durables	12
(14) Fuel and utilities	nil

SOURCE: A. P. Barten, "Consumer Demand Functions under Conditions of Almost Additive Preferences," *Econometrica* 32, no. 1–2 (January–April 1964): 9.

4.3.3.1 Zero Restrictions on Elasticity Components. As we have seen, the three components of price elasticity are related to each other, and to income elasticities, by a variety of constraints. It is obvious that certain nondiagonal elements of $\boldsymbol{G}_2$ will vanish whenever the corresponding element of $\boldsymbol{U}^{-1}$ vanishes—these elements will vanish if an appropriate subset of elements in

[27] Barten, "Consumer Demand Functions . . .," op. cit.

U vanishes; that is, provided the "right" commodities in U are independent. *It is at this point that the concept of almost additive preferences pays off.* The definition (2.45) implies that nonzero off-diagonal elements in U^{-1} occur in the *same* positions as in U. Consequently we have established the following important result (due to Barten):

> *Under almost additive preferences, whenever two commodities are independent their cross "specific" substitution effects vanish.*

That is, for any pair i and j belonging to different preference blocks,

$$\eta_{2ij} = 0 \qquad \begin{cases} i \in \text{block } r \\ j \notin \text{block } r \end{cases} \tag{4.67}$$

The total number of off-diagonal elements of G_2 is $k(k-1)$. However, from (4.67), some of these are known to be zero. Indeed, if q_i is the number of other commodities with which, according to the prior specification, commodity i may interact, then $(k-q_i-1)$ off-diagonal terms in the ith rows of G_2, $\hat{W}G_2$ and $G_2^T\hat{W}$, are zero. The total number of elements in G_2 set a priori to zero, then, is $\Sigma_i(k-q_i-1)$; that is, $k(k-1)-\Sigma q_i$. The remaining elasticities ticities must be estimated; these number $k^2-[k(k-1)-\Sigma q_i]$, that is, $[k+\Sigma q_i]$. The total number of elasticities to be estimated, after taking account of information about the block structure of preferences, can now be tallied up. First, there are k income elasticities. Then there are the $2k^2$ components of price elasticity contained in G_1 and G_3. Finally, there are the $[k+\Sigma q_i]$ elasticities of G_2. Noting that Σq_i is the sum of the number of interacting pairs in each block, we can conclude as follows.

> Consider a consumer's utility function which is block-independent, almost additive. Let there be n blocks, with $v(l)$ commodities contained in the lth block ($l=1,\ldots,n;\ n<k$). Then the number of components of price elasticity η_{2ij} due to specific substitution effects that may be nonzero is
>
> $$k + \sum_{l=1}^{n} \{v(l)[v(l)-1]\} \tag{4.68a}$$
>
> or
>
> $$k + \sum_{i=1}^{k} q_i \tag{4.68b}$$
>
> where q_i is the number of commodities with which commodity number i is allowed to interact.[28]

[28] When applying (4.68b), keep in mind that under the specification being discussed, commodity i is allowed to interact with every other commodity contained within the same block. If, as in Table 4.1, certain within-block interactions are set to zero, formula (4.68b) will give the correct total, which will be lower than that indicated by (4.68a).

4.3.3.2 Dimensionality of the Parameter Space. We are now in a position to make explicit the dimensionality of the parameter space to be estimated. In terms of our elasticity formulation, we started with $k+3k^2$ parameters to be estimated; namely, the income elasticity vector $\boldsymbol{E}$ and the price elasticity matrices $\boldsymbol{G}_1$, $\boldsymbol{G}_2$, and $\boldsymbol{G}_3$. The progressive elimination of parameters due to *additivity*, *homogeneity*, *block-independent almost additivity*, and *symmetry* are as set out in Table 4–2. The final two constraints contributing to the shrinkage of the parameter space are the systematic relationship of the *income effect* and the *general substitution effect* to income derivatives. The total number of independent parameters to be estimates, $k+\frac{1}{2}\Sigma q_i$, may be thought

Table 4–2

Dimensionality of Parameter Space Under Block-Independent Almost Additive Preferences

Description	Number of Elasticities	Reference: Eqn. No.
Unconstrained System	(a): $k + 3k^2$	(4.48), (4.32)
No. parameters eliminated due to *additivity* of expenditures to income.	1	(4.44)
No. parameters eliminated due to *relationship between specific substitution effects and income derivatives* (or, alternatively, due to *homogeneity* of the demand function).	$k - 1$	(4.36)
No. parameters eliminated due to *relationship between income derivatives and general substitution effect.*	k^2	(4.45)
No. parameters eliminated due to *relationship between income derivatives and the income effect* of a price change.	k^2	(4.46)
No. parameters eliminated due to *block-independent almost additivity* of preference function.	$k(k-1) - \sum_{i=1}^{k} q_i$	(4.47)
No. parameters eliminated due to *symmetry* of substitution effects	$\frac{1}{2}\sum_{i=1}^{k} q_i$	(4.55)
Total no. parameters eliminated.	(b): $3k^2 - \frac{1}{2}\sum_{i=1}^{k} q_i$	
Dimension of parameter space to be estimated (before trends are added to system).	(a) – (b): $k + \frac{1}{2}\sum_{i=1}^{k} q_i$	

of as follows: $(k-1)$ independent income responses, one Frisch "money flexibility" parameter, and $\frac{1}{2}\Sigma q_i$ specific substitution components of price elasticity. The "price" paid for allowing specific interactions to occur—that is, the price of going from directly additive preferences to block-independent almost additive preferences—is that these $\frac{1}{2}\Sigma q_i$ specific interactions must be estimated.

The dimension of the parameter space in the case of block-independent almost additive preferences is very similar to that under the specification that certain substitution elasticities are zero. One may enquire, then, what advantages the use of Barten's prior specification has over the assumption that certain partial substitution elasticities are zero. [For, as can be seen from (3.99), estimation in the latter case would be straightforward.] The answer runs in terms of economic plausibility. If partial substitution elasticities are zero, the entire substitution effect must vanish. In the two-commodity world, this implies right-angled indifference curves and a "fixed coefficient" utility function (reminiscent of the Leontief production function). Barten's specification—that the marginal utility of some goods is unaffected by the consumption levels of others—makes better economic sense.

4.3.3.3 Estimation Scheme. The block-independent almost additive specification tells us that

$$\eta_{2ij} = \lambda h_{ij}(u_{ii}u_{jj})^{-1/2}p_j/x_i \qquad (i \neq j) \tag{4.69}$$

[where we have used (4.33b) and (2.48)] for all i and j. By definition,

$$h_{ij} = 0 \qquad \begin{cases} \text{for } i \text{ and } j\ (i \neq j) \\ \text{from } \textit{different} \text{ preference} \\ \text{blocks.} \end{cases} \tag{4.70}$$

The diagonal elements of $\boldsymbol{G}_2$ are as in (4.63); namely $\omega^{-1}E_i$. Using (4.62), (4.69) reduces to

$$\eta_{2ij} = \omega^{-1}h_{ij}(w_j^\circ/w_i^\circ)^{1/2}(E_iE_j)^{1/2} \qquad (i \neq j) \tag{4.71}$$

where the identity from (4.62) has been enforced at the set of budget shares $\{w_i^\circ\}$.

The estimation problem is to find ω, the nonvanishing h_{ij}'s, and $\boldsymbol{E}$. After substitution from (4.71) and (4.63) into (4.50c), a system of equations displaying extreme nonlinearity in the parameters is obtained. The appropriate computational procedures for such a system are outside the scope of this book.[29]

---

[29] Barten ("Consumer Demand Functions . . .," op. cit.) gives details of a fitting procedure. A more general survey of approaches to fitting nonlinear systems is given by S. M. Goldfeld and R. E. Quandt, *Non-Linear Methods in Econometrics* (Amsterdam: North-Holland, 1972).

5 An Extension in Parameter Space: Brown and Heien's *S*-Branch Utility Tree

5.1 The *S*-Branch Utility Tree[1]

As we have seen in Chapter 3, since the Stone-Geary utility function is directly additive, there are no specific substitution effects in the Linear Expenditure System (LES). Neither is there room in that system for complementarity or for inferior goods, nor for price elasticities whose absolute values exceed unity. Brown and Heien have modified Sato's two-level CES production function[2] to obtain the utility function which they term the "*S*-branch utility tree." In the demand system associated with this utility function, specific substitution effects do not necessarily vanish. Complementarity is possible (but under restricted conditions); more importantly, own-price elasticities are free to vary in the interval $(0, -\infty)$. Finally, the *S*-branch utility tree contains the LES as a special case. Relative to the LES, these generalizations are achieved at the cost of introducing an additional *S* parameters, where *S* is the number of branches (or blocks) into which the arguments of the utility function is partitioned.

The *S*-branch utility function is written

$$u(x) = \left\{ \sum_{s=1}^{S} \alpha_s \left[\sum_{i \in s}^{n_s} \beta_{si} (x_{si} - \gamma_{si})^{\rho_s} \right]^{\rho/\rho_s} \right\}^{1/\rho} \tag{5.1}$$

in which s is an index identifying the sth among the S blocks $\{\boldsymbol{x}_1, \ldots, \boldsymbol{x}_s\}$ into which the k commodities are partitioned $(S < k)$; i is an index identifying the ith commodity within the sth block $(i = 1, 2, \ldots, n_s)$; n_s is the number of commodities in the sth block of the partition

$$\left(\text{thus } \sum_{s=1}^{S} n_s \equiv k\right)$$

[1] This chapter closely follows Murray Brown and Dale Heien, "The S-Branch Utility Tree: A Generalization of the Linear Expenditure Function," *Econometrica* 40, no. 4 (July 1972): 737–747.

[2] K. Sato, "A Two-Level Constant Elasticity of Substitution Production Function," *Review of Economic Studies* 34, no. 98 (April 1967): 201–218.

and γ_{si} is a "subsistence" quantity parameter for good i within block s (analogous to γ_i in the LES). The parameters α_s reflect the importance of the different blocks in generating total utility; the β_{si}, on the other hand, reflect the importance (in generating utility) of particular commodities within given blocks. The α's, β's, and γ's are all assumed to be positive. The parameters $\{\rho_1, ..., \rho_s\}$ and ρ are related to substitution elasticities $\{\sigma_1, ..., \sigma_S\}$ and σ as follows:

$$\rho = 1 - 1/\sigma \qquad (\rho < 1, \text{ by assumption}) \tag{5.2a}$$

$$\rho_s = 1 - 1/\sigma_s \qquad (\rho_s < 1;\ s = 1, ..., S, \text{ by assumption}) \tag{5.2b}$$

The interpretation of these partial substitution elasticities is in terms of "above subsistence" or "supernumerary" quantities $\{(x_{si} - \gamma_{si})\}$. In fact, if $\sigma_{si,rj}$ is the partial elasticity of substitution between the supernumerary quantity of good i in block s and the supernumerary quantity of good j in block r, then it can be shown that

$$\sigma_{si,rj} = \sigma \qquad (\text{if } s \neq r) \tag{5.3a}$$

$$= \sigma + \frac{1}{w_s}(\sigma_s - \sigma) \qquad (\text{if } s = r) \tag{5.3b}$$

where

$$w_s = \frac{\sum_{j \in s} p_{sj}(x_{sj} - \gamma_{sj})}{m - \sum_{r=1}^{S} \sum_{i \in r} p_{ri}\gamma_{ri}} \tag{5.3c}$$

with p_{sj} (for example) denoting the price of the jth commodity in the sth block; and m (as before) denoting total consumption expenditure.[3]

Brown and Heien note that while (5.1) is a utility tree, it satisfies the even stronger property of block additivity. This is easily verified by replacing the utility index u of (5.1) by its monotonic transform

$$u^* = (u)^\rho \tag{5.4}$$

Then the functional form of u^* clearly satisfies the block additivity requirement (2.2).

[3] These results are completely analogous with those for the standard partial substitution elasticities in the case of the two-level CES production function. See K. Sato, op. cit.

5.2 Demand Functions

The separability properties of (5.1) imply that maximization within blocks does not depend on quantities from other blocks, except insofar as these affect total spending on the block in question.[4] Selecting an arbitrary expenditure level m_s for allocation among the n_s items of block s, maximization of

$$u_s = \sum_{i \in s} \beta_{si}(x_{si} - \gamma_{si})^{\rho_s} \tag{5.5a}$$

subject to

$$\sum_{i \in s} p_{si} x_{si} = m_s \tag{5.5b}$$

yields the preliminary demand functions

$$x_{si} = \gamma_{si} + (\beta_{si}/p_{si})^{\sigma_s}\left[\sum_{j \in s} (\beta_{sj}/p_{sj})^{\sigma_s} p_{sj}\right]^{-1} \cdot \left[m_s - \sum_{j \in s} p_{sj}\gamma_{sj}\right] \tag{5.6}$$

Upon substitution of these values into (5.1), a "premaximized" utility function (analogous to a concentrated likelihood function) is obtained:

$$u^{\circ} = \left\{\sum_{r=1}^{S} \alpha_r X_r^{-\rho(1-1/\rho_r)} M_r^{\rho}\right\}^{1/\rho} \tag{5.7a}$$

where

$$X_r = \sum_{j \in r} (\beta_{rj}/p_{rj})^{\sigma_r} p_{rj} \tag{5.7b}$$

and

$$M_r = m_r - \sum_{j \in r} p_{rj}\gamma_{rj} \tag{5.7c}$$

The maximization problem is completed by maximizing (5.7a) subject to the budget constraint,

$$m = \sum_{r=1}^{S} m_r = \sum_{r=1}^{S} \sum_{j \in r} p_{rj} x_{rj} \tag{5.7d}$$

The optimal values of M_r are found by conventional methods:

$$M_r = [\alpha_r^{\sigma} X_r^{(\sigma-1)/(\sigma_r-1)}]\left[\sum_{s=1}^{S} \alpha_s^{\sigma} X_s^{(\sigma-1)/(\sigma_s-1)}\right]^{-1} \cdot \left(m - \sum_{s=1}^{S} \sum_{j \in s} p_{sj}\gamma_{sj}\right) \tag{5.8}$$

[4] W. M. Gorman, "Separable Utility and Aggregation," *Econometrica* 27, no. 3 (July 1959): 469–481; R. H. Strotz, "The Utility Tree—A Correction and Further Appraisal," *Econometrica* 27, no. 3 (July 1959): 482–488.

From (5.7c), (5.8), and (5.7b), m_s can be found in terms of prices $\{p_{sj}\}$, total expenditure m, and the parameters of the model. The full S-branch demand functions are found by substituting this value of m_s into (5.6). After simplification, these demand functions are

$$x_{si} = \gamma_{si} + (\beta_{si}/p_{si})^{\sigma_s}[\alpha_s^{\sigma} X_s^{[(\sigma-1)/(\sigma_s-1)]-1}]$$

$$\times\left(m - \sum_{r=1}^{S} \sum_{j\in r} p_{rj}\gamma_{rj}\right)\cdot\left[\sum_{r=1}^{S} \alpha_r^{\sigma} X_r^{(\sigma-1)/(\sigma_r-1)}\right]^{-1} \tag{5.9}$$

Suppose $S = 1$. Then (5.9) reduces to the one-level modified CES form:

$$x_i = \gamma_i + (\beta_i/p_i)^{\sigma_1}\left[\sum_{j=1}^{k} (\beta_j/p_j)^{\sigma_1} p_j\right]^{-1} \cdot \left(m - \sum_{j=1}^{k} p_j\gamma_j\right) \tag{5.10}$$

where the s subscript has been suppressed (except in the case of σ_1, which would otherwise be indistinguishable from σ). Putting $\sigma_1 = 1$ yields the linear expenditure system.

The modified CES utility function for $S = 1$, and its associated demand functions, are termed by Brown and Heien "the S_0-Branch System."[5] This system has been investigated by Christensen, Pollak, and Gamaletsos.[6] The last mentioned has dubbed (5.10) the *generalized linear expenditure system.*

For empirical work, Brown and Heien reject the S_0-branch system, because of the specification that the substitution elasticities between all pairs $\{(x_i-\gamma_i), (x_j-\gamma_j)\}$ of supernumerary quantities share a common value, σ_1. On the other hand, allowing $\sigma_1 \neq 1$ represents a significant advance in flexibility over the LES, since own price elasticities may now vary in the interval $(0, -\infty)$. As in the LES, complements and inferior goods are ruled out in the S_0-branch system. Moreover, the S-branch system and all of its special cases involve linear Engel curves [see (5.9)]. Brown and Heien refer to the version of their system in which $S > 1$ as the S_1-branch system.

---

[5] Brown and Heien, op. cit.

[6] Christensen investigated the CES utility function in the intertemporal setting. See Laurits Ray Christensen, "Savings and the Rate of Return," Ph.D. thesis, University of California, Berkeley 1967, available as Systems Formulation, Methodology and Policy Workshop Paper 6805, Social Systems Research Institute, University of Wisconsin, 1968. R. A. Pollak, "Additive Utility Functions and Linear Engel Curves," University of Pennsylvania, Department of Economics Discussion Paper no. 53, June 1967 (revised February 1968). Theodore Gamaletsos, "Further Analysis of Cross Country Comparison of Consumer Expenditure Patterns," *European Economic Review* 4, no. 1 (April 1973): 1–20.

5.3 Slutsky Derivatives

Let $\kappa_{si,rj}$ be the Slutsky compensated cross-price derivative of good i in block s with respect to the price of good j in block r. Brown and Heien give expressions for two types of Slutsky derivatives: (i) for goods in different blocks, and (ii) for goods in the same block. These are

$$\kappa_{si,rj} = \frac{(x_{si}-\gamma_{si})(x_{rj}-\gamma_{rj})\,\sigma}{(m-\sum_{r'=1}^{S}\sum_{j\in r'} p_{r'j}\gamma_{r'j})} \qquad (\text{for } r \neq s) \tag{5.11a}$$

$$\kappa_{si,rj} = \frac{(x_{si}-\gamma_{si})(x_{sj}-\gamma_{sj})\,\sigma}{(m-\sum_{r'=1}^{S}\sum_{j\in r'} p_{r'j}\gamma_{r'j})} - \frac{(x_{si}-\gamma_{si})(\sigma-\sigma_s)(x_{sj}-\gamma_{sj})}{(m_s-\sum_{i'\in s} p_{si'}\gamma_{si'})}$$

$$(\text{for } r = s,\ i \neq j) \tag{5.11b}$$

For the utility function u to be everywhere defined, we require (as in the LES) that supernumerary quantities and supernumerary expenditure be positive. Given that $\sigma > 0$, the intergroup Slutsky derivatives (5.11a) are, therefore, uniformly positive. Any two commodities from different blocks are hence substitutes. In (5.11b), the term $(\sigma-\sigma_s)$ may be positive, negative, or zero. Hence it is possible for two commodities belonging to the same block to be complements.

5.4 Price and Income Elasticities

The expenditure elasticities E_{si} in all versions of the S-branch system are

$$E_{si} = \frac{x_{si}-\gamma_{si}}{x_{si}} \cdot \frac{m}{(m-\sum_{r=1}^{S}\sum_{j\in r} p_{rj} x_{rj})} \tag{5.12}$$

In the case of the LES, $S = 1$, $\sigma_1 = 1$, and (5.12) reduces to the expression shown in the fourth line of Table 3–1. Own-price elasticities have also been derived by Brown and Heien as[7]

$$\eta_{si,si} = -\frac{(x_{si}-\gamma_{si})}{x_{si}}\left[w_{si}+\sigma(W_{si}-w_{si})+\sigma_s W_{si}\right] \tag{5.13a}$$

in which

$$w_{si} = \frac{p_{si}(x_{si}-\gamma_{si})}{(m-\sum_{r=1}^{S}\sum_{j\in r} p_{rj}\gamma_{rj})} \tag{5.13b}$$

and

$$W_{si} = \frac{p_{si}(x_{si}-\gamma_{si})}{(m_s-\sum_{j\in s} p_{sj}\gamma_{sj})} \tag{5.13c}$$

[7] Brown and Heien, op. cit., p. 742.

The expressions w_{si} and W_{si} share the same numerator. The denominator of W_{si} is supernumerary expenditure from the sth block; it must be less than the overall supernumerary expenditure which is the denominator of w_{si}. Hence W_{si} exceeds w_{si}, and (5.13a) is unambiguously negative. Suitable variations of the parameters $\{\gamma_{rj}; r = 1, \ldots, S; j \in r\}$, σ and σ_s will generate values of $\eta_{si,si}$ in the interval $(0, -\infty)$. Note that the parameters $\{\alpha_s\}$ and $\{\beta_{si}\}$ do not appear explicitly in (5.13a). In empirical work, however, the observed x values will not correspond exactly with the values generated by the fitted values of the systems parameters and the values of the exogenous variables at which the elasticities are to be estimated. To estimate the elasticities in a way strictly consistent with the systems postulates it is necessary to substitute for x_{si} in (5.12) and (5.13a) from (5.9). The expressions so obtained *do* involve α's and β's. The only variables appearing, however, are the exogenous set of prices $\{p_{si}\}$ and total expenditure, m.

5.5 Outline of Estimation Procedures

Brown and Heien opted for an additive error appended to the expenditure equations obtained by multiplying (5.9) through by p_{si}. As with the LES of Chapter 3, the error terms are postulated to have classical serial properties. Nonzero contemporaneous covariances are allowed, both between errors for commodities in the same block; and between errors for commodities from different blocks. The (by now) familiar problem of singularity of the contemporaneous covariance matrix is again encountered, and is handled by methods similar to those discussed in Chapter 3. Following Pollak and Wales, Brown and Heien also introduced habit formation into the determination of a time path of γ_{si}'s rather than keeping these as fixed parameters.[8] The maximum-likelihood method was implemented using Bard's algorithm.[9] The Gauss-Newton search procedure and analytic (rather than numeric) derivatives were employed within this algorithm. Brown and Heien report empirical results for a three-way split of food expenditure into Meat (with Fish, Beef, Poultry, and Pork as components), Vegetables (with 6 subcategories distinguished), and Fruits (also disaggregated into 6 components). The authors claim that the S_1-branch system "can be estimated with little or no more effort than that expended on the linear expenditure system." Insufficient experience has so far accrued, however, to know whether this will in fact turn out to be the case.

---

[8] R. A. Pollak and T. J. Wales, "Estimation of the Linear Expenditure System," *Econometrica* 37, no. 4 (October 1969): 611–628. See Section 3.4.1 above.

[9] Y. Bard, "Non-Linear Parameter Estimation and Programming," I.B.M. Contributed Program Library 360D–13.6.003 (December 1967).

6 Endogenizing Savings[1]

All of the models so far discussed have treated total consumption expenditure as predetermined. The convenient fiction adopted has been that of a two-level decision-making process, whose first stage involves the trade-off between now and later, and whose second stage involves trade-offs among the consumption opportunities of the present. In this chapter, the intertemporal and the intercommodity aspects of decision making are unified. The predetermined variables driving this new system are time paths of prices and of income; the endogenous quantities are the time paths of expenditure on different items, plus the time path of saving.[2] The micro (i.e., household-level) consumption function is seen as the sum over commodities of its commodity expenditure functions.

6.1 Early Foundations—Tintner

In the post-Fisherian period, the dawn of modern intertemporal utility-maximizing models is usually put at Ramsey's 1928 article on optimal savings.[3] Probably influenced by this development, Tintner, in two papers appearing in 1938, considered the intertemporal problem of a consumer faced with given expectations about prices, income, and interest rates over a finite planning horizon of length n. The problem was formulated both in discrete time and in continuous time.[4]

---

[1] Without implicating him in remaining errors, I would like to thank Arthur Goldberger for reading and commenting on Section 6.2.4 of this chapter.

[2] The latter is just the difference between predetermined income and the sum of the (endogenous) consumption expenditures.

[3] F. P. Ramsey, "A Mathematical Theory of Saving," *Economic Journal* 38, no. 152 (December 1928): 543–559.

[4] Gerhard Tintner, "The Maximization of Utility over Time," *Econometrica* 6, no. 2 (1938): 154–158; "The Theoretical Derivation of Dynamic Demand Curves," *Econometrica* 6, no. 4 (1938): 375–380.

6.1.1 *Discrete Time Formulation*

In the discrete time case the utility function is written without any assumption of separability in time; i.e., utility generated over the plan is written

$$U = F(\boldsymbol{x}_1, \boldsymbol{x}_2, \ldots, \boldsymbol{x}_n) \tag{6.1}$$

in which $\boldsymbol{x}_\tau$ ($\tau = 1, \ldots, n$) is the k vector of quantities of different goods consumed in period τ. Total expenditure expected to occur in planning period τ is

$$\boldsymbol{p}_\tau^T \boldsymbol{x} = m_\tau \tag{6.2}$$

while expected savings are

$$s_\tau = I_\tau - m_\tau \tag{6.3}$$

I_τ being expected income (which is exogenous in this model). Writing i_τ as the (exogenous) interest rate expected in planning period τ, the life-time budget constraint is written *in flow terms* by Tintner as

$$\begin{aligned} I_1 &= m_1 + s_1 \\ I_2 + s_1(1+i_1) &= m_2 + s_2 \\ \vdots \qquad \vdots \\ I_n + s_{n-1}(1+i_{n-1}) &= m_n \end{aligned} \tag{6.4}$$

[Terminal savings are set to zero—bequests do not appear in the utility function (6.1).] The constrained maximization problem to be solved is the maximization of (6.1) subject to (6.4). For this, n Lagrange multipliers λ_τ are introduced to accommodate the restrictions (6.4). The endogenous variables of the system are $nk+2n-1$ in number, being the nk quantities to be consumed in the plan, the n Lagrange multipliers giving the marginal utilities (from the viewpoint of the beginning of the plan) of a marginal dollar optimally spent in periods $1, 2, \ldots, n$; and the $n-1$ amounts saved. Differentiation of the Lagrangean gives $nk+2n-1$ necessary conditions,

$$\underset{k\times 1}{\frac{\partial F}{\partial \boldsymbol{x}_\tau}} = \underset{k\times 1}{\lambda_\tau \boldsymbol{p}_\tau} = \underset{k\times 1}{\boldsymbol{0}} \qquad (\tau = 1, \ldots, n) \tag{6.5a}$$

$$-\lambda_\tau + \lambda_{\tau+1}(1+i_\tau) = 0 \qquad (\tau = 1, 2, \ldots, n-1) \tag{6.5b}$$

{Budget constraint over life of plan as expressed in (6.4)} (6.5c)

Tintner manipulates these first order conditions to derive some very meaningful economic relationships among the variables; he does not, however, suggest any particularizations of F nor any other route for making the system empirically estimable. Finally, he gives the stock equivalent of the constraints (6.4),

$$I_1 + \sum_{l=2}^{n} I_l \prod_{\tau=1}^{l-1} (1+i_\tau)^{-1} = m_1 + \sum_{l=2}^{n} m_l \prod_{\tau=1}^{l-1} (1+i_\tau)^{-1} \tag{6.6}$$

i.e.,

$$PV(\text{income stream}) = PV(\text{expenditure stream}) \tag{6.7}$$

[in which $PV(\ )$ is "present value of ( )"], and remarks that treating (6.6) rather than (6.4) as the subsidiary condition makes no difference.

The discrete time problem has now an established place in the literature, at least as a theoretical tool. A comprehensive textbook treatment is given by Hadar, who gives in addition a bibliographic history of the subject (including a treatment of the continuous time problem).[5] Empirical applications have been rare; a recent example of the application of the discrete time model is given by Weber.[6]

6.1.2 Continuous Time Formulation

For his continuous time treatment of the problem, Tintner uses the budget constraint in stock form (rather than flow form); i.e., he uses the continuous analogue of (6.6),

$$\int_0^n I(t') \exp\left[-\int_0^{t'} \rho(\tau)\, d\tau\right] dt' = \int_0^{t'} m(t') \exp\left[-\int_0^{t'} \rho(\tau)\, d\tau\right] dt' \tag{6.8}$$

[where on the LHS $\exp(\ )$ = the exponential function] which allows for the possibility of a functional dependence of the instantaneous discount factor

$$r(t') = \exp\left[-\int_0^{t'} \rho(\tau)\, d\tau\right] \tag{6.9}$$

[5] Josef Hadar, *Mathematical Theory of Economic Behavior* (Reading, Mass.: Addison-Wesley, 1971), pp. 209–249.

[6] Warren E. Weber, "Interest Rates, Relative Prices, and Consumer Expenditures for Durables and Non-Durables: A Multiperiod Utility Maximization Approach," Department of Economics, Virginia Polytechnic and State University, Blacksburg, Virginia, February 1972.

on planning time t'. The problem is treated by Tintner as a calculus-of-variations problem in which the maximand is the functional

$$U = f[\boldsymbol{x}(t')]_0^n \tag{6.10}$$

which, since it does not even assume intertemporal additivity of utilities, is a very general statement of the problem indeed. The first-order conditions are shown to be

$$\frac{f'_{x_i(t')}}{p_i(t')} = \Lambda r(t') \tag{6.11}$$

in which only a scalar Euler-Lagrange multiplier, Λ, is involved, and where $x_i(t')$, $p_i(t')$ are the ith elements of $\boldsymbol{x}(t')$ and $\boldsymbol{p}(t')$ respectively, and $f'_{x_i(t')}$ is the *functional* derivative of f with respect to the *function* $x_i(t')$ at point t'.

Again, Tintner did not attempt to specialize the utility functional f. He did, however, consider restrictions implied by the maximization procedure for demand functions (under both the continuous and discrete formulations).[7] The relationships derived, though important and open to clear economic interpretation, did not lead to empirically implementable models apparently until the work of Modigliani and Brumberg (1954), Lluch (1970), and Weber (1972).[8]

6.2 Lluch's Extended Linear Expenditure System (ELES)

6.2.1 Continuous Time with Intertemporally Additive Utility Functional

In his 1970 paper, Lluch works in continuous time.[9] As in the case of Tintner, price expectations over the plan are taken as given. Income from two sources is distinguished, however; from endowments of human and nonhuman wealth.[10] Two interest rates enter the formulation rather than one. These are

---

[7] Tintner, "The Theoretical Derivation of Dynamic Demand Curves," op. cit.

[8] The implementation by Modigliani and Brumberg was limited in scope to a one-commodity model. See F. Modigliani and R. Brumberg, "Utility Analysis and the Consumption Function: An Interpretation of Cross Section Data," in K. K. Kurihara, Ed., *Post Keynesian Economics* (New Brunswick: Rutgers University Press, 1954), pp. 388–436. Constantino Lluch, "The Extended Linear Expenditure System," University of Essex Discussion Paper no. 16 (February 1970); a revised version has been published under the same title in *European Economic Review* 4, no. 1 (1973): 21–32. Warren Weber, op. cit.

[9] Lluch, op. cit.

[10] Only one accumulation relationship; namely, that for nonhuman wealth, is treated explicitly in the model.

the pure time-preference rate (δ) and the market rate of interest (ρ). The latter, by virtue of the assumption of perfect capital markets, is identically the rate of return on holdings of wealth in nonhuman form. The two interest rates δ and ρ are assumed to be constant over the life of a consumption plan $\{\boldsymbol{x}(\tau)\}$. Whilst Fisherian equilibrium requires the equality of δ and ρ, within Lluch's framework it is necessary that ρ exceed δ if certain integrals are to converge.[11]

Three particularizations adopted by Lluch lead to a great simplification in the analysis. The first is intertemporal additivity of the utility functional. The second is that the instantaneous utility function is stationary. The third is that the time-preference discount rate is constant. Taken together these imply that the abstract maximand of (6.10) can be replaced with a present value of the utility stream; namely,

$$U = \int_0^n e^{-\delta\tau} u[\boldsymbol{x}(\tau)]\, d\tau \tag{6.12}$$

in which $u[\ ]$ is the instantaneous utility function which is supposed to depend only on time rates of consumption of the various k items in the budget. [Thus the ith element of $\boldsymbol{x}(\tau)$, namely, $x_i(\tau)$, is the rate at which item i is expected (from the planning viewpoint) to be consumed at the notional instant $\tau (0 \le \tau \le n)$.] The consumer's intertemporal choice problem is seen to be that of maximizing (6.12) subject to:

i. an exogenously given expected labor earnings stream $\{y(\tau)\}$, representing the yield on the initially given endowment of human wealth;
ii. an exogenously given expected time path for commodity prices $\{\boldsymbol{p}(\tau)\}$, which are assumed stationary over the plan $[\boldsymbol{p}(\tau) \equiv \boldsymbol{p}$ for $0 \le \tau \le n]$;
iii. an initial endowment $w(0)$ of wealth held in nonhuman form;
iv. a terminal (nonhuman) wealth target, $w(n)$;
v. the following accumulation relationship for nonhuman wealth (hereinafter abbreviated simply to "wealth"):

$$\dot{w}(\tau) = \rho w(\tau) + y(\tau) - \boldsymbol{p}^T \boldsymbol{x}(\tau) \tag{6.13}$$

in which $\dot{w}(\tau)$ is $d[w(\tau)]/d\tau$.

Finally, we require all consumption flows to be non-negative:

$$\dot{x}_i(\tau) \ge 0 \qquad (0 \le \tau \le n;\ i = 1, \ldots, k) \tag{6.14}$$

[11] Within a more general framework it is necessary for ρ to exceed δ if consumption along the optimal path is to increase. See Menahem E. Yaari, "On the Consumer's Lifetime Allocation Process," *International Economic Review* 5, no. 3 (September 1964): 309.

To simplify matters further, bequests are eliminated by specifying $w(n) = 0$. The initial conditions and the accumulation relationship (6.13) are equivalent to a lifetime budget constraint which can be written in terms of the following stock balance:

$$\boldsymbol{p}^T \int_0^n \boldsymbol{x}(\tau) e^{-\rho\tau} d\tau = w(0) + \int_0^n y(\tau) e^{-\rho\tau} d\tau \tag{6.15}$$

which states that the present value of planned expenditures should equal initial net worth; viz., the sum of initial wealth plus discounted labor earnings over the plan.

Lluch gives the following first-order (Euler-Lagrange) conditions for determining the optimum demand functions $\boldsymbol{x}(\tau)$:[12]

$$\frac{\partial u}{\partial \boldsymbol{x}(\tau)} = \lambda(\tau) e^{\delta\tau} \boldsymbol{p} \tag{6.16a}$$

and

$$\frac{d\lambda(\tau)}{d\tau} = -\rho\lambda(\tau) \tag{6.16b}$$

In addition, of course, the initial and terminal conditions, as well as (6.13)—or, equivalently, (6.15)—must be satisfied. In (6.16a) are represented the derivatives of instantaneous utility with respect to the k consumption flows, $x_i(\tau)$. The function $\lambda(\tau)$ is a Euler-Lagrange multiplier. According to (6.16b), $\lambda(\tau)$ declines over the plan at a constant geometric rate equal to the market rate of interest. From (6.16a) Lluch derives what he terms "the basic differential equation system of demand theory":

$$\dot{\boldsymbol{x}}(\tau) = \lambda(0)(\delta - \rho) e^{(\delta-\rho)\tau} \boldsymbol{U}^{-1} \boldsymbol{p} \tag{6.17}$$

in which $\boldsymbol{U}$ is the Hessian of the instantaneous utility function.[13]

---

[12] The unknowns of the calculus of variation problem here described are the *functions* $\boldsymbol{x}(\tau)$. The arguments of these (demand) functions become clear later.

[13] Constantino Lluch, "Systems of Demand Functions under Intertemporal Utility Maximization," *University of Essex, Department of Economics Discussion Paper* no. 11 (January 1970), mimeo. See also Constantino Lluch and Michio Morishima, "Demand for Commodities Under Uncertain Expectations," ch. 5 in M. Morishima, Ed., *Theory of Demand, Real and Monetary* (New York: Oxford University Press, 1973).

In the case of an infinite planning horizon ($n \to \infty$), the first-order conditions reduce to

$$\frac{\partial u}{\partial \boldsymbol{x}(\tau)} = \lambda(0)e^{(\delta-\rho)\tau}\boldsymbol{p} \tag{6.18a}$$

$$\boldsymbol{p}^T L(\boldsymbol{x}) = L(y) + w(0) \tag{6.18b}$$

in which L is the Laplace transform; i.e., the present-value operator which discounts the notional streams $\{\boldsymbol{x}(\tau);\, 0 \leq \tau < \infty\}$ and $\{y(\tau);\, 0 \leq \tau < \infty\}$ to the present at the discount rate ρ. (Note that $L(\boldsymbol{x})$ is a k-dimensional vector of present "values" of time derivatives of quantities.) Focussing attention on the initial instant of planning time ($\tau = 0$), (6.18a and b) become[14]

$$\frac{\partial u}{\partial \boldsymbol{x}(0)} = \lambda(0)\boldsymbol{p} \tag{6.19a}$$

$$\boldsymbol{p}^T\boldsymbol{x}(0) = y(0) + L(\dot{y}) + \rho w(0) - \boldsymbol{p}^T L(\dot{\boldsymbol{x}}) \tag{6.19b}$$

Introducing

$$z(0) = y(0) + \rho w(0) + L(\dot{y}) \tag{6.19c}$$

a more convenient notation for (6.19b) is

$$\boldsymbol{p}^T\boldsymbol{x}(0) = z(0) - \boldsymbol{p}^T L(\dot{\boldsymbol{x}}) \tag{6.19d}$$

Paraphrasing Lluch to accommodate notational differences:

> System (6.19a) is identical with the set of marginal conditions in static demand theory. The "budget constraint" (6.19b) contains the difference between the intertemporal utility maximization model with endogenous savings and the usual (i.e., static) formulation. In fact the former problem reduces to the latter if the optimal consumption plan and expected labor income flow are stationary—i.e., if $L(\dot{y}) = 0 = L(\dot{\boldsymbol{x}})$.[15]

By envisaging actual behavior as a series of initial instants $\{t = 0\}$ of infinite optimal plans, these equations can be used to generate behavioral relationships if the instantaneous utility function $u[\boldsymbol{x}(\tau)]$ is given a particular functional form.[16]

---

[14] In deriving (6.19b) an elementary property of Laplace transforms, $\{L(f') = \rho L(f) - f(0)\}$, has been used.

[15] Constantino Lluch, "The Extended Linear Expenditure System," *European Economic Review*, op. cit., p. 25.

[16] Lluch has investigated several functional forms for u; see Constantino Lluch, "Functional Form for Utility, Demand Systems, and the Aggregate Consumption Function," *IEEE Transactions on Automatic Control*, AC-18, no. 4 (August 1973): 385–387.

6.2.2 Stone-Geary Instantaneous Utility Function

The derivation of the extended linear expenditure system (ELES) from the necessary conditions (6.19a and b) and from (6.17) straightforward. Putting

$$u[\boldsymbol{x}(\tau)] = \sum_{i=1}^{k} \beta_i \log[x_i(\tau)-\gamma_i] \qquad (0<\beta_i<1;\ i=1,\ldots,k) \tag{6.20}$$

we have that

$$\frac{\partial u}{\partial x_i(\tau)} = \frac{\beta_i}{x_i(\tau)-\gamma_i} \tag{6.21a}$$

whose matrix representation is

$$\frac{\partial u}{\partial \boldsymbol{x}(\tau)} = [\hat{\boldsymbol{x}}(\tau)-\hat{\boldsymbol{\gamma}}]^{-1}\boldsymbol{\beta} \tag{6.21b}$$

in which $\hat{\boldsymbol{x}}(\tau)$ and $\hat{\boldsymbol{\gamma}}$ are, respectively, the diagonal matrices with diagonal elements $x_i(\tau)$ and γ_i respectively; and where $\boldsymbol{\beta}$, as in Chapter 3, contains the k marginal budget shares. Under this specification, Lluch has demonstrated that (6.17) reduces to

$$\dot{\boldsymbol{x}}(\tau) = (\rho-\delta)[\boldsymbol{x}(\tau)-\boldsymbol{\gamma}] \tag{6.22}$$

in which $\boldsymbol{\gamma}$ is as in Chapter 3.[17] Applying the operator L to both sides of (6.22), making a substitution based on the property of L that

$$L(\dot{\boldsymbol{x}}) = \rho L(\boldsymbol{x}) - \boldsymbol{x}(0)$$

we obtain after simplification:

$$L(\dot{\boldsymbol{x}}) = (\mu^{-1}-1)(\boldsymbol{x}(0)-\boldsymbol{\gamma}) \tag{6.23}$$

in which, by definition,

$$\mu = (\delta/\rho) \tag{6.24}$$

[17] Lluch, "The Extended Linear Expenditure System," op. cit. Since $\dot{\boldsymbol{x}}(\tau) \equiv d[\boldsymbol{x}(\tau)-\boldsymbol{\gamma}]/d\tau$, (6.22) states that "above subsistence" quantities grow in the optimal plan at a constant geometric rate $(\rho-\delta)$.

Using (6.21b) in (6.18a) and (6.23) in (6.19d), we obtain

$$[\hat{\boldsymbol{x}}(0)-\hat{\boldsymbol{\gamma}}]^{-1}\boldsymbol{\beta} = \lambda(0)\boldsymbol{p} \tag{6.25a}$$

and

$$\boldsymbol{p}^T\boldsymbol{x}(0) = (1-\mu)\boldsymbol{p}^T\boldsymbol{\gamma} + \mu z(0) \tag{6.25b}$$

These are $(k+1)$ equations in an equal number of unknowns, $\boldsymbol{x}(0)$ and $\lambda(0)$. The solution for $x_i(0)$ is

$$p_i x_i = p_i \gamma_i + \mu\beta_i[z(0)-\boldsymbol{p}^T\boldsymbol{\gamma}] \tag{6.26a}$$

which has as its matrix representation

$$\hat{\boldsymbol{p}}\boldsymbol{x}(0) = \hat{\boldsymbol{p}}\boldsymbol{\gamma} + \mu\boldsymbol{\beta}[z(0)-\boldsymbol{p}^T\boldsymbol{\gamma}] \tag{6.26b}$$

in which $\hat{\boldsymbol{p}}$ is the diagonal matrix formed from $\boldsymbol{p}$. This system is Lluch's *extended linear expenditure system* (ELES). If we now drop planning time (τ) as an argument of $\boldsymbol{x}$ and z, and regard historic time as a succession of initial instants $\tau = 0$, then (6.26b) may be rewritten

$$\hat{\boldsymbol{p}}_t\boldsymbol{x}_t = \hat{\boldsymbol{p}}_t\boldsymbol{\gamma} + \mu\boldsymbol{\beta}[z_t-\boldsymbol{p}_t^T\boldsymbol{\gamma}] \tag{6.27}$$

in which t is real time and its use as a subscript identifies sample realizations.

Because the distinction between planning time and historical time is so crucial in this model, it may do no harm to labor the point: the representative consumer whose behavior at moment t of historical time is portrayed by (6.27) is assumed by construction to be *continually* at the initial point of an optimal consumption plan of infinite length.[18] Thus it is supposed that the consumer is continually revising his optimal plan. Although at historical instant t he plans as if prices $\{\boldsymbol{p}_t\}$ then prevalent will last forever, at instant $(t+\Delta)$ he will substitute a new set of stationary prices $\{\boldsymbol{p}_{t+\Delta}\}$ if prices change between t and $(t+\Delta)$. Changes in expectations about labor income will also lead to revisions in the optimal plan. It is true, however, that such a consumer would find himself at $(t+\Delta)$ on the plan seen as optimal from viewpoint t if prices and the variable z_t at $(t+\Delta)$ turned out in fact to be exactly the same as at instant t.

---

[18] The substitution of a finite planning period for an infinite one would only have a small impact on the structure of the problem except where the interest rates involved are very low or where the planning horizon is very short. For the U.S. economy in the postwar period, Heien estimates that the consumption planning horizon for the "representative consumer" is in excess of twenty years—see Dale Heien, "Demographic Effects and the Multiperiod Consumption Function," *Journal of Political Economy* 80, no. 1 (January–February 1972): 125–138.

The variable z_t in (6.27) is [from (6.19c)]

$$z_t = y_t + \rho w_t + L_t(\dot{y}) \tag{6.28a}$$

$$= Y_t + L_t(\dot{y}) \tag{6.28b}$$

in which $L_t(\dot{y})$ is the present value of changes expected in labor income as seen from instant t of historic time, and in which Y_t is actual income (from both labor and capital) at instant t. Thus z_t is readily identified as a *permanent income* concept, consisting of actual income plus the present value of changes expected to accrue in labor income. Since there is no room in the model for gains in nonhuman capital, z_t puts all accumulated lifetime expected earnings on a flow basis.

The microconsumption function appropriate to the representative consumer is obtained by adding (6.27) across commodities. Writing m_t as total consumption at t, we obtain

$$m_t = (1-\mu)\boldsymbol{p}^T\gamma + \mu z_t \tag{6.29}$$

which is a restatement of (6.25b). Solving (6.29) for z_t, and substituting back into (6.27), we obtain

$$\hat{\boldsymbol{p}}_t \boldsymbol{x}_t = \hat{\boldsymbol{p}}_t \gamma + \boldsymbol{\beta}[m_t - \boldsymbol{p}_t^T \gamma] \tag{6.30}$$

which is just Stone's LES (3.5). This shows that, considerations of stochastic elements aside, the LES is fully consistent with ELES. The econometric complications arise because, within the ELES frame of reference, (6.30) has the *endogenous* variable m_t on the right-hand side.

6.2.3 Elasticities in ELES

Only very slight modifications to the LES formula are required for the (permanent) income elasticity and the price elasticities in ELES. Using superscripts ° to indicate arbitrarily chosen values of the exogenous variables $\{\boldsymbol{P}; z\}$, and indicating corresponding values of endogenous variables likewise, we have

(PERMANENT) INCOME ELASTICITY

$$E_i = \mu\beta_i \frac{z^\circ}{p_i^\circ x_i^\circ} \tag{6.31}$$

UNCOMPENSATED PRICE ELASTICITIES

$$\text{Own } (i=j)\text{: } \eta_{ii} = (1-\mu\beta_i)\frac{\gamma_i}{x_i^\circ} - 1 \tag{6.32a}$$

$$\text{Cross } (i \neq j)\text{: } \eta_{ij} = -\mu\beta_i \frac{\gamma_j p_j^\circ}{p_i^\circ x_i^\circ} \tag{6.32b}$$

To define compensated price elasticities it is first necessary to define a utility-compensating increment in real income with which to sterilize the income effect of an increment dp in prices.

As reference point we take (expected) prices and permanent income streams to be stationary: from planning viewpoint t,

$$p_{it}(\tau) \equiv p_{it} \qquad (\tau \geq t) \tag{6.33a}$$

$$z_t(\tau) \equiv z_t \tag{6.33b}$$

in which $p_{it}(\tau)$ is the price expected to prevail for good i at instant τ from planning viewpoint t ($t \leq \tau$); p_{it} is historic price; and similar definitions apply to z.

Write $x_{it}(\tau)$ for consumption of i planned for τ from viewpoint t. Under these conditions the optimal plan is exponential in supernumerary quantities:

$$\begin{aligned} x_{it}(\tau) - \gamma_i &= [x_{it}(t) - \gamma_i]\, e^{(\rho-\delta)(\tau-t)} \qquad (6.34) \\ &= (x_{it} - \gamma_i)\, e^{(\rho-\delta)(\tau-t)} \qquad (\tau \geq t) \end{aligned}$$

which is the solution to Lluch's differential equation (6.22).[19]

The indirect utility functional is obtained by substituting (6.34) into

$$U_t = \int_0^\infty e^{-\delta\tau'} \sum_{i=1}^{k} \beta_i \log[x_{it}(\tau) - \gamma_i]\, d\tau' \tag{6.35}$$

where $\tau' \equiv \tau - t$, and then making the substitution,

$$x_{it} = \gamma_i + \mu\beta_i(z_t - \boldsymbol{p}_t^T \gamma)/p_{it} \tag{6.36}$$

Upon doing so, and keeping in mind that

$$\sum_{i=1}^{k} \beta_i \equiv 1$$

[19] Lluch, "The Extended Linear Expenditure System," op. cit.

we obtain

$$U_t = \sum_{i=1}^{n} \beta_i \log[\mu\beta_i(z_t - \boldsymbol{p}_t^T\gamma)/\mathrm{p}_{it}] \int_0^\infty e^{-\delta\tau'}\, d\tau' + (\rho-\delta)\int_0^\infty e^{-\delta\tau'}\tau'\, d\tau'$$

$$= \delta^{-1}\left[\sum_{i=1}^{k} \beta_i \log\mu\beta_i + \sum_{i=1}^{k} \beta_i \log(z_t - \boldsymbol{p}_t^T\gamma) - \sum_{i=1}^{k} \beta_i \log p_{it}\right] + \text{constant} \qquad (6.37)$$

Take differentials of both sides, set $dU_t = 0$, multiply both sides by δ, and solve for the differential in z which sterilizes a differential $d\boldsymbol{p} = (dp_1, \ldots, dp_k)$ in prices:

$$\sum_{i=1}^{k} \beta_i (z_t - \boldsymbol{p}_t^T\gamma)^{-1}\, d(z_t - \boldsymbol{p}_t^T\gamma) = \sum_{i=1}^{k} \beta_i (p_{it})^{-1}\, dp_{it} \qquad (6.38)$$

That is,

$$(z_t - \boldsymbol{p}_t^T\gamma)^{-1} \cdot \sum_{i=1}^{k} \beta_i \cdot dz_t = (z_t - \boldsymbol{p}_t^T\gamma)^{-1} \sum_{i=1}^{k} \beta_i \gamma^T\, d\boldsymbol{p}_t + \sum_{i=1}^{k} \beta_i (p_{it})^{-1}\, dp_{it} \qquad (6.39)$$

Keeping in mind

$$\sum_{i=1}^{k} \beta_i \equiv 1$$

and multiplying by $(z_t - \boldsymbol{p}_t^T\gamma)$, we get

$$dz_t = \gamma^T\, d\boldsymbol{p}_t + (z_t - \boldsymbol{p}_t^T\gamma)\, \boldsymbol{\beta}^T\, \boldsymbol{d}\,\mathbf{log}\,\boldsymbol{p}_t \qquad (6.40)$$

Allow only one price to change; i.e., put all elements of $\boldsymbol{dp}_t$ and $\boldsymbol{d}\,\mathbf{log}\,\boldsymbol{p}_t = 0$ except for the jth in each case.

$$dz_t = \gamma_j\, dp_{jt} + (z_t - \boldsymbol{p}_t^T\gamma)\frac{\beta_j}{p_{jt}}\, dp_{jt}$$

$$= G_j(\boldsymbol{p}_t, z_t)\, dp_{jt} \qquad \text{(say)} \qquad (6.41)$$

The ELES demand functions are (say)

$$x_{it} = F^i(\boldsymbol{p}_t, z_t)$$

$$= \gamma_i + \frac{\mu\beta_i(z_t - \boldsymbol{p}_t^T\gamma)}{p_{it}} \qquad (6.42)$$

Taking total differentials (but again with all prices other than the jth held constant):

$$dx_{it} = \frac{\partial F^i}{\partial p_{jt}} dp_{jt} + \frac{\partial F^i}{\partial z_t} dz_t \tag{6.43}$$

For dz_t, substitute from (6.41):

$$dx_{it} = \left[\frac{\partial F^i}{\partial p_{jt}} + \frac{\partial F^i}{\partial z_t} G_j\right] dp_{jt} \tag{6.44}$$

The utility-compensated derivative of commodity i with respect to price j is found by taking dp_{jt} to the LHS. For $i \neq j$,

$$\left.\frac{dx_{it}}{dp_{jt}}\right|_{\text{Compensated}} = \frac{\partial F^i}{\partial p_{jt}} + \frac{\partial F^i}{\partial z_t} G_j$$

$$= \mu \beta_i \beta_j (z_t - \boldsymbol{p}_t^T \gamma)/(p_{it}\, p_{jt}) \tag{6.45}$$

$$= \beta_i \beta_j (v_t - \boldsymbol{p}_t^T \gamma)/(p_{it}\, p_{jt}) \tag{6.46}$$

which is identically the same as in LES. For $i = j$ we obtain

$$\left.\frac{dx_{it}}{dp_{it}}\right|_{\text{Compensated}} = -\mu \beta_i (z_t - \boldsymbol{p}_t^T \gamma)(1 - \beta_i)/(p_{it})^2$$

$$= -\beta_i (v_t - \boldsymbol{p}_t^T \gamma)(1 - \beta_i)/(p_{it})^2 \tag{6.47}$$

as in LES. In elasticity form, these are identical with the LES compensated elasticities ε_{ij}° shown in Table 3–1.

6.2.4 Estimation of ELES

6.2.4.1 Error Structure. The formulation sketched above is deterministic. As such, it lacks any econometric dimension. The most sophisticated approaches to the *static* demand problem involve building stochastic elements into the utility function.[20] While intellectually satisfying because of the unity they achieve between their econometric and the economic dimensions, even in the

---

[20] See, e.g., Anton Barten, "Estimating Demand Equations," *Econometrica* 36, no. 2 (April 1968): 213–351; R. A. Pollak and Terence J. Wales, "Estimation of the Linear Expenditure System," *Econometrica* 37, no. 4 (October 1969): 611–628.

static case such models are not easily implemented. In the case of the dynamic problem of this chapter, the economic methodology would go from calculus of variations to stochastic control theory. Here we will not be this ambitious, preferring to add a zero-mean stochastic element to the final behavioral relations. If e_{it} is this random element in the case of the tth observation for the ith equation of (6.27), we write[21]

$$v_{it} \equiv p_{it} x_{it} = p_{it} \gamma_i + \mu \beta_i (z_t - \mathbf{p}_t^T \gamma) + e_{it} \tag{6.48}$$

where we suppose

$$E(e_{it}) = 0 \qquad \text{(for all } i, t\text{)} \tag{6.49a}$$

$$E(e_{it} e_{j\tau}) = 0 \qquad \text{(for all } t \neq \tau, \text{ all } (i, j)\text{)} \tag{6.49b}$$

$$E(e_{it} e_{j\tau}) = \sigma_{ij} \qquad \text{otherwise} \tag{6.49c}$$

Writing

$$\mathbf{\Sigma} = [\sigma_{ij}] \tag{6.50}$$

there is no reason to suppose $\mathbf{\Sigma}$ is singular: expenditures, after all, do not add identically to permanent income. This framework is fully consistent with the traditional formulation of the error structure for the LES. Summing (6.48) over i to obtain m_t on the left, solving this expression for $(z_t - \mathbf{p}_t^T \gamma)$, and substituting the value so obtained back into (6.48), we obtain

$$v_{it} = p_{it} \gamma_i + \beta_i (m_t - \mathbf{p}_t^T \gamma) + (e_{it} - \beta_i \mathbf{1}^T \mathbf{e}_t) \tag{6.51}$$

This is just (6.30) apart from the error term,

$$e_{it}^* = (e_{it} - \beta_i \mathbf{1}^T \mathbf{e}_t) \equiv e_{it} - \beta_i \sum_{j=1}^{k} e_{jt} \tag{6.52}$$

Since $\mathbf{1}^T \boldsymbol{\beta} \equiv 1$, it is easy to see that $\mathbf{1}^T \mathbf{e}_t^* \equiv 0$, and consequently that the covariance matrix for the errors in the LES is singular (as in Chapter 3). However, (6.52) gives a rationalization for this singularity which goes beyond accounting necessity. We are also able to write an expression for this singular covariance structure in terms of the full rank structure $\mathbf{\Sigma}$:

$$E(\mathbf{e}_t^*)(\mathbf{e}_t^*)^T = \mathbf{\Sigma} + (\mathbf{1}^T \mathbf{\Sigma} \mathbf{1}) \cdot \boldsymbol{\beta} \boldsymbol{\beta}^T - \boldsymbol{\beta} \mathbf{1}^T \mathbf{\Sigma} - \mathbf{\Sigma} \mathbf{1} \boldsymbol{\beta}^T \qquad \text{(all } t\text{)} \tag{6.53}$$

---

[21] In (6.48) we work with the discrete time analogue of (6.26b).

In what follows we put aside till a later section the vexing question of how data on z_t might be obtained, concentrating on the estimation problem of ELES in its own right.

6.2.4.2 Maximum-Likelihood Estimation: Time Series. Analogous to the systems format (3.38a) for the LES (and in the same notation) is

$$\begin{bmatrix} \boldsymbol{v}_1 \\ \boldsymbol{v}_2 \\ \vdots \\ \boldsymbol{v}_k \end{bmatrix} = \left[\begin{array}{cccc:cccc} \boldsymbol{p}^1 & \mathbf{0} & \cdots & \mathbf{0} & (\boldsymbol{z}-\boldsymbol{P}\gamma) & \mathbf{0} & \cdots & \mathbf{0} \\ \mathbf{0} & \boldsymbol{p}^2 & \cdots & \mathbf{0} & \mathbf{0} & (\boldsymbol{z}-\boldsymbol{P}\gamma) & \cdots & \mathbf{0} \\ \vdots & & & & \vdots & & & \\ \mathbf{0} & \mathbf{0} & \cdots & \boldsymbol{p}^k & \mathbf{0} & \mathbf{0} & \cdots & (\boldsymbol{z}-\boldsymbol{P}\gamma) \end{array}\right] \begin{bmatrix} \gamma_1 \\ \gamma_2 \\ \vdots \\ \gamma_k \\ \hline \mu\beta_1 \\ \mu\beta_2 \\ \vdots \\ \mu\beta_k \end{bmatrix} + \begin{bmatrix} \boldsymbol{e}_1 \\ \boldsymbol{e}_2 \\ \vdots \\ \boldsymbol{e}_k \end{bmatrix} \tag{6.54}$$

Note that no truncation of this system has been carried out. If we identify the vector $(\mu\boldsymbol{\beta})$ above with the *truncated* vector $\boldsymbol{\beta}^{\circ}$ of the LES, and γ of ELES with (the identical) γ in LES, then there is a striking isomorphism between the full-rank LES subsystem after truncation, and with ELES. It follows that both systems may be estimated by identical methods. Whereas in LES $(k-1)$ β_i's are estimated, and the remaining coefficient found from the restriction

$$\beta_l = 1 - \sum_{j \neq l} \beta_j \tag{6.55}$$

in ELES, the k elements of $\mu\boldsymbol{\beta}$ are estimated and μ found from

$$\sum_{i=1}^{k} (\mu\beta_i) \equiv \mu \tag{6.56}$$

Only one very slight dimensional difference between LES and ELES prevents LES software (such as LINEX[22]) being used for the estimation of ELES. Whereas in ELES the $(\mu\boldsymbol{\beta})$ vector and the γ vector are of the same order, and this integer is equal to the number of equations in the system, in LES the γ vector contains one more element than the $\boldsymbol{\beta}^{\circ}$ vector, whose order is equal to

---

[22] F. Carlevaro and E. Rossier, "Le Programme Linex Pour L'Estimation des Parametres Du Systeme Lineaire De Depenses," Faculte des Sciences Economiques et Sociales, Universite de Geneve, Centre D'Econometrie, Cahier, 15 June, 1970.

the number of equations in the full-rank subsystem.[23] Under the assumption of joint normality of the e_{it}'s, the mathematics of the maximum likelihood estimation of ELES is identical with that of LES; consequently the work of Parks and Solari is fully adequate, apart from matters of fine detail.[24] (See Chapter 3.)

6.2.4.3 Maximum-Likelihood Estimation: Cross Sections.[25] *Permanent Income Known Accurately*. For the moment we continue to assume that data on z_t are available. In the case of cross-sectional data it is rare for any variation in prices to occur.[26] Recasting the analysis to reflect this, we write

$$v_{it} = \Theta_i + \Phi_i z_t + e_{it} \qquad (i = 1, \ldots, k) \qquad (6.57a)$$

in which

$$\Theta_i = p_i \gamma_i - \mu \beta_i \boldsymbol{p}^T \boldsymbol{\gamma} \qquad (p_{it} \equiv p_i, \boldsymbol{p}_t \equiv \boldsymbol{p}, \text{ all } t) \qquad (6.57b)$$

and

$$\Phi_i = \mu \beta_i \qquad (6.57c)$$

Equation (6.57a) is the "identical regressors" problem in which every left-hand variable is regressed on the same set of exogenous variables $[\mathbf{1}, \boldsymbol{z}]$. Under

[23] Since *every* γ_i appears in *each* expenditure equation of the LES, its truncation by one equation does not lead to the disappearance of any γ_i.

[24] Richard Parks, "Maximum Likelihood Estimation of the Linear Expenditure System," *Journal of the American Statistical Association* 66, no. 336, Theory and Methods Section (December 1971): 900–903; and Luigi Solari, *Theori des Choix et Fonctions de Consommation Semi-Agregées, Modeles Statistiques* (Geneva: Dros, 1971). At the date of writing, only two instances of the maximum likelihood fitting of ELES had been completed: namely, Constantino Lluch and Ross Williams, "Consumer Demand Systems and Aggregate Consumption in the U.S.A.: An Application of the Extended Linear Expenditure System," Development Research Center, World Bank, Washington, D.C. (May 1973), mimeo; and (by the same authors), "Cross Country Demand and Savings Patterns: An Application of the Extended Linear Expenditure System," Development Research Center, World Bank, Washington, D.C. (July 1973) mimeo. These authors did not attempt to use LINEX because of the difficulties involved in making even slight alterations to a highly compact and sophisticated program; rather they used Bard's IBM software for extremizing an arbitrary function.

[25] Based largely on Alan Powell, "The Estimation of Lluch's Extended Linear Expenditure System from Cross Section Data," *Australian Journal of Statistics* 15, no. 2 (August 1973). Many ideas presented here were developed either implicitly or explicitly by Francisco Belandria in "An Empirical Study of Consumer Expenditure Patterns in Venezuelan Cities," Ph.D. dissertation, Northwestern University, August 1971.

[26] For an exception, see Lluch's analysis of inter-regional price differentials: Constantino Lluch, "Consumer Demand Functions, Spain, 1958–1964," *European Economic Review* 2, no. 3 (Spring 1971): 277–302.

the assumption that the e_{it} are joint normally distributed, the full-information maximum-likelihood estimates of ELES can therefore be obtained by the use of ordinary least squares applied to (6.57a) on a commodity-by-commodity basis.[27]

As we have seen, the consumption function obtained by summing the commodity expenditure equations (6.48) is

$$m_t = (1-\mu)\boldsymbol{p}^T\gamma + \mu z_t + \mathbf{1}^T\boldsymbol{e}_t \tag{6.58}$$

The variance of the disturbance in this equation is, from (6.50),

$$\text{var}\,(\mathbf{1}^T\boldsymbol{e}_t) = \mathbf{1}^T\boldsymbol{\Sigma}\mathbf{1} \tag{6.59}$$

The maximum-likelihood estimate of μ is obtainable by adding the OLS estimates of the Φ_i's:

$$\hat{\mu} = \sum_{i=1}^{n} \hat{\Phi}_i = \mathbf{1}^T\hat{\boldsymbol{\Phi}} \tag{6.60}$$

where the restriction $(\sum_{i=1}^{n} \beta_i \equiv 1)$ has been used.[28] The maximum-likelihood estimates of the marginal budget shares β_i are then obtainable as

$$\hat{\beta}_i = \hat{\Phi}_i/\mathbf{1}^T\hat{\boldsymbol{\Phi}} \tag{6.61}$$

In the cross-sectional context, adding the estimated Θ's across equations gives

$$\text{MLE of } \{(1-\mu)\boldsymbol{p}^T\gamma\} = \mathbf{1}^T\hat{\boldsymbol{\Theta}} \tag{6.62}$$

The maximum-likelihood estimate of $(\boldsymbol{p}^T\gamma)$ is obtained as

$$\text{MLE of } (\boldsymbol{p}^T\gamma) = \frac{\mathbf{1}^T\hat{\boldsymbol{\Theta}}}{1-\mathbf{1}^T\hat{\boldsymbol{\Phi}}} \tag{6.63}$$

---

[27] A. S. Goldberger, *Econometric Theory* (New York: Wiley, 1964), pp. 207–212; Phoebus Dhrymes, *Econometrics—Statistical Foundations and Applications* (New York: Harper & Row, 1970), pp. 153–161.

[28] This $\hat{\mu}$ is identically the estimate of μ obtained by the single equation regression (6.58) of m_t on z_t (which justifies the ML interpretation of (6.60)). Similarly, the expression given in (6.62) is identically the estimate of $(\mathbf{1}^T\boldsymbol{\Theta})$ which would be obtained from the single equation regression (6.58). In equations (6.63) and (6.64), on the other hand, 1:1 transformations from one parameter set into another are involved, and hence the invariance theorem on ML estimators may be used.

Finally, estimates of $(p_i \gamma_i)$ are obtained from expression (6.57b) as

$$\text{MLE of } (p_i \gamma_i) = \hat{\Theta}_i + \frac{\hat{\Phi}_i \mathbf{1}^T \hat{\boldsymbol{\Theta}}}{1 - \mathbf{1}^T \hat{\boldsymbol{\Phi}}} \tag{6.64}$$

Notice that it is not necessary to have price variation over the subscript t in order to identify the γ_i's; it is necessary to have *measurements* on the p_i (that is, of the prices of the k different consumption items).

The asymptotic variances of the various MLE's may be obtained by observing that estimates of the small sample variances and covariances of $\hat{\Theta}_i$ and $\hat{\Phi}_i$ are

$$\underset{2\times 2}{\text{Est. } \mathbf{var}} \begin{bmatrix} \hat{\Theta}_i \\ \hat{\Phi}_i \end{bmatrix} = \frac{\hat{\sigma}_i^2}{N \sum_{t=1}^N z_t^2 - (\sum_{t=1}^N z_t)^2} \begin{bmatrix} \sum_{t=1}^N z_t^2 & -\left(\sum_{t=1}^N z_t\right) \\ -\left(\sum_{t=1}^N z_t\right) & N \end{bmatrix} \tag{6.65}$$

in which N is sample size and $\hat{\sigma}_i^2$ is the mean of the squared residuals from an OLS fit of (6.57a). Use is then made of the standard result relating the asymptotic variance of a function of a random vector to the derivatives of that function and the asymptotic variance-covariance matrix of that random vector.[29]

Permanent Income Data Unavailable. Two other results for the estimation of ELES from cross-sectional data may be summarized as follows:

a. If, because permanent income data are not available, the LES-based equations

$$v_{it} = \alpha_i + \beta_i m_t + e_{it}^* \tag{6.66}$$

are fitted instead of (6.57a), the large sample bias[30] in the OLSE of $\hat{\beta}_i$ is

$$\text{LSB}(\hat{\beta}_i) = \frac{\mathbf{1}^T \boldsymbol{\sigma}_i - \beta_i \mathbf{1}^T \boldsymbol{\Sigma} \mathbf{1}}{\mu^2 \operatorname{var}(z_t) + (1-\mu)^2 \boldsymbol{\gamma}^T V \boldsymbol{\gamma} + \mathbf{1}^T \boldsymbol{\Sigma} \mathbf{1}} \tag{6.67}$$

in which $\boldsymbol{\sigma}_i$ is the ith column of $\boldsymbol{\Sigma}$ and V is the variance-covariance matrix of prices, assumed stationary.[31]

---

[29] Goldberger, op. cit., p. 125.

[30] That is, difference between probability limit and parameter value.

[31] Powell, op. cit. The exogenous variables $\boldsymbol{P}$ and $\boldsymbol{z}$, if stochastic, are assumed to have sample covariances with $\boldsymbol{e}$ which vanish in the probability limit. The sample covariances of $\boldsymbol{z}$ with $\boldsymbol{P}$ are also assumed to vanish in the probability limit.

b. Since the OLS estimators $\hat{\beta}_i$ obtained from (6.66) add identically to unity, both their small and large sample biases add across commodities to zero. Consequently, it may be possible to partition the sample data to obtain a number of estimates of each β_i in such a way that for any particular β_i the biases incurred in different subsamples have offsetting signs. Averaging the $\hat{\beta}_i$'s across subsamples may then go a long way toward removing the biases.[32]

Zellner and Goldberger's Unobservable Variables Approach.[33] Commonly, in cross-sectional (i.e., household) studies, observations are collected on socioeconomic and demographic variables which allow detailed modelling of permanent income. If this collection of variables after (probably a large number of) suitable transformations is labelled $\boldsymbol{Z}_t$ for the tth household, then we may suppose

$$z_t = \boldsymbol{Z}_t^T \boldsymbol{\alpha} + w_t \qquad (6.68)$$

in which $\boldsymbol{\alpha}$ is a $g \times 1$ vector giving the structural coefficients relating to permanent income the variables which jointly "explain" its systematic component. To be fully concrete, we suppose that in (6.68) a regression constant is involved, so that the leading element of each $\boldsymbol{Z}_t$ is a unit, there being $(g-1)$ relevant socioeconomic/demographic variables.

The problem of estimating *an equation* such as (6.57a) in conjunction with a permanent income generator of the type (6.68) has been investigated by Goldberger;[34] however, only under the condition that $\Theta_i \equiv 0$. The problem of handling the entire *system* of which (6.57a) is a typical equation has also been investigated by Goldberger under the same assumption ($\Theta_i \equiv 0$ all i).[35] This assumption, unfortunately, plays a crucial role in the analysis of the problem. What can be given here is a sketch of how Goldberger's ML approach might proceed—full details remain to be worked out.

The reduced form of the expenditure equations is obtained by substituting (6.68) for z_t in (6.57a):

$$v_{it} = \Theta_i + \Phi_i(\boldsymbol{Z}_t^T \boldsymbol{\alpha}) + (e_{it} + \Phi_i w_t) \qquad (i = 1, \ldots, k) \qquad (6.69)$$

[32] Alan Powell, "The Analysis of Synoptic Cross-Section Data on Consumer Budgets," Development Research Center, World Bank, Washington, D.C. (September 1972) (mimeo).

[33] Arnold Zellner, "Estimation of Regression Relationships Containing Unobservable Variables," *International Economic Review* 11 (October 1970): 441–454; A. S. Goldberger, "Maximum Likelihood Estimation of Regressions Containing Unobservable Independent Variables," *International Economic Review* 13, no. 1 (February 1972), 1–15.

[34] Goldberger, "Maximum Likelihood Estimation . . .," op. cit.

[35] Ibid.

If α_j is the jth element of $\boldsymbol{\alpha}$, and we define $\boldsymbol{\alpha}_i^*$ as the vector whose last $(g-1)$ elements are the same as those of $\boldsymbol{\alpha}$, but whose first element is

$$\alpha_{i1}^* \equiv \Theta_i/\Phi_i + \alpha_1 \tag{6.70}$$

then (6.69) may be written

$$v_{it} = \Phi_i(\boldsymbol{Z}_t^T\boldsymbol{\alpha}_i^*) + (e_{it}+\Phi_i w_t) \qquad (i=1,\dots,k) \tag{6.71}$$

In a slightly more conventional notation, (6.71) is

$$[v_{1t},\dots,v_{kt}] = \boldsymbol{Z}_t^T[\boldsymbol{\pi}_1,\dots,\boldsymbol{\pi}_k] + [r_{1t},\dots,r_{kt}] \tag{6.72a}$$

that is,

$$\boldsymbol{v}_t^T = \boldsymbol{Z}_t^T\boldsymbol{\Pi} + \boldsymbol{r}_t^T \tag{6.72b}$$

in which

$$\boldsymbol{\pi}_i \equiv \Phi_i\boldsymbol{\alpha}_i^* \tag{6.73a}$$

and

$$r_{it} \equiv e_{it} + \Phi_i w_t \tag{6.73b}$$

Following Zellner and Goldberger, the exogenous variables $\boldsymbol{Z}_t$ are taken as nonstochastic.[36] Their sample moment matrix is taken to be of full rank; namely g. Note that the elements of the $g\times k$ matrix $\boldsymbol{\Pi}$ are restricted by the requirement that the subvector containing the last $(g-1)$ elements of any column i is a scalar multiple (Φ_i/Φ_j) of the corresponding subvector of column j. (Thus the rank of $\boldsymbol{\Pi}$ is 2.) Also notice that r_{it} will be correlated with r_{jt} $(i\neq j)$, since both involve realizations on the same random variable w_t. We assume the covariance matrices for the r_{it}'s are the same for all households t; that is, we assume that

$$E(\boldsymbol{r}_t\boldsymbol{r}_t^T) = \boldsymbol{R} \qquad (\text{all } t) \tag{6.74}$$

We have the

$$(i,j)\text{th element of } E(\boldsymbol{r}_t\boldsymbol{r}_t^T) = E\{e_{it}e_{jt}+\Phi_j e_{it}w_t+\Phi_i e_{jt}w_t+\Phi_i\Phi_j w_t^2\} \tag{6.75}$$

---

[36] Zellner, "Estimation of Regressions . . .," op. cit.; Goldberger, "Maximum Likelihood Estimation . . .," op. cit.

Besides independence between the e's and the w's, we assume that the equation errors e_{it} and w_t are distributed without sequential correlation across the household index t. Hence (6.75) becomes, the

$$
\begin{aligned}
(i, j)\text{th element of } E(\boldsymbol{r}_t \boldsymbol{r}_\tau^T) &= \sigma_{ij} + \Phi_i \Phi_j \sigma_w^2 \qquad (\text{if } t = \tau) \\
&= 0 \qquad (\text{otherwise}) \qquad (6.76)
\end{aligned}
$$

where σ_w^2 is the variance of w_t (assumed constant). In matrix terms,

$$\mathbf{R} = \mathbf{\Sigma} + \sigma_w^2 \mathbf{\Phi}\mathbf{\Phi}^T \qquad (6.77)$$

In what follows, we shall write

$$\boldsymbol{Y} = \begin{bmatrix} v_{11} & \cdots & v_{k1} \\ v_{12} & \cdots & v_{k2} \\ \vdots & & \vdots \\ v_{1N} & \cdots & v_{kN} \end{bmatrix} \qquad (6.78a)$$

and

$$\boldsymbol{Z} = \begin{bmatrix} \boldsymbol{Z}_1^T \\ \boldsymbol{Z}_2^T \\ \vdots \\ \boldsymbol{Z}_N^T \end{bmatrix} \qquad (6.78b)$$

as the data matrices for the reduced form. Under the assumption that the e's and the w's are normal, the log likelihood function for the reduced form (6.72a and b) is

$$L(\boldsymbol{\Pi}, \boldsymbol{R}; \boldsymbol{Y}, \boldsymbol{Z}) = \text{constant} - \frac{N}{2} \log |\boldsymbol{R}| - \frac{N}{2} \operatorname{trace}(\boldsymbol{R}^{-1} \boldsymbol{A}) \qquad (6.79a)$$

in which $\boldsymbol{A}$ is the k-order square matrix,

$$\boldsymbol{A} = \frac{1}{N} (\boldsymbol{Y} - \boldsymbol{Z}\boldsymbol{\Pi})^T (\boldsymbol{Y} - \boldsymbol{Z}\boldsymbol{\Pi}) \qquad (6.79b)$$

The subset of first-order conditions for the maximum of (6.79a) obtained by differentiating L with respect to the elements of $\boldsymbol{R}$, lead to the standard result

$$\boldsymbol{R} = \boldsymbol{A} \qquad (6.80)$$

The concentrated likelihood function, therefore, is

$$L^c = \text{constant} - \frac{N}{2}\log|\boldsymbol{A}| \tag{6.81}$$

Hence the ML problem is that of minimizing $\log|\boldsymbol{A}|$ with respect to the structural parameters.[37] These are $\boldsymbol{\alpha}$, $\boldsymbol{\Theta}$, $\boldsymbol{\Phi}$, $\boldsymbol{\Sigma}$ and σ_w^2. The conditions for the identification of this model have only been worked out under the condition $\boldsymbol{\Theta} = \boldsymbol{0}$; even in that case, a further constraint (namely that $\boldsymbol{\Sigma}$ is diagonal) is needed to achieve full identification.[38] Further work is needed. However, a simple count of unknowns does not make for optimism in the case of the present problem.

Goldberger also investigates the case in which $\sigma_w^2 = 0$; i.e., permanent income is a nonstochastic function of the socioeconomic/demographic variables.[39] In that case (but with $\boldsymbol{\Theta} = \boldsymbol{0}$), the model is identified even if $\boldsymbol{\Sigma}$ is not diagonal. If we put $\sigma_w^2 = 0$ into (6.77), we see that no restrictions [other than positive semidefiniteness, required by (6.80) and (6.79b)] are placed on $\boldsymbol{R}$. If we write out the reduced form coefficient matrix $\boldsymbol{\Pi}$, in full, we obtain

$$\underset{g \times k}{\boldsymbol{\Pi} = [\pi_{ij}]} = \begin{bmatrix} \boldsymbol{\Pi}_1^T \\ \hdashline \boldsymbol{\Pi}_2 \end{bmatrix} = \begin{bmatrix} \pi_{11} & \cdots & \pi_{1k} \\ \hdashline \boldsymbol{\pi}_2^1 & \cdots & \boldsymbol{\pi}_2^k \end{bmatrix}$$

$$= \begin{bmatrix} \Theta_1 + \Phi_1 \alpha_1 & \cdots & \Theta_k + \Phi_k \alpha_1 \\ \hdashline \Phi_1 \boldsymbol{\alpha}^\circ & \cdots & \Phi_k \boldsymbol{\alpha}^\circ \end{bmatrix} \tag{6.82}$$

in which $\boldsymbol{\alpha}^\circ$ is the last $(g-1)$ elements of both $\boldsymbol{\alpha}$ and each $\boldsymbol{\alpha}_i^*$. The only binding restriction on the reduced form is that $\boldsymbol{\Pi}_2$ should have unit rank. This is the type of restriction which (as Goldberger remarks[40]) is very familiar in the theory of the identification of linear econometric models. The limited-information maximum-likelihood procedure (LIML) is well adapted to handle rank restrictions on submatrices of $\boldsymbol{\Pi}$. Hence a LIML program might

---

[37] It must be kept in mind that the concentrated likelihood already involves setting k^2 derivatives to zero, each of which involves $\boldsymbol{\Phi}$, $\boldsymbol{\Sigma}$, and σ_w^2. To obtain the full list of first-order conditions, L^c may be differentiated with respect to $\boldsymbol{\alpha}$ and $\boldsymbol{\Theta}$; in the other cases, it is L that must be differentiated.

[38] Goldberger, "Maximum Likelihood Estimation . . .," op. cit.

[39] Ibid.

[40] Ibid.

be adapted to produce full information ML estimates of the ELES cross-section reduced form when the permanent income generator is nonstochastic.[41] Assume that this estimation has been carried out. Then, by construction, the estimates $\{\hat{\pi}_{lh}\}$ will have the property that, *for any fixed pair* $\{i, j\}$,

$$\hat{\pi}_{lj}/\hat{\pi}_{li} = \text{constant} \qquad (\text{all } l = 2, \ldots, g) \tag{6.83}$$

Also, recalling the definition that $\Phi_i \equiv \mu\beta_i$, we see that

$$\beta_i = \left[\sum_{j=1}^{k} \Phi_j/\Phi_i\right]^{-1} \tag{6.84}$$

where we have used the fact that $\mathbf{1}^T\boldsymbol{\beta} = 1$. But from (6.82),

$$\hat{\pi}_{lj}/\hat{\pi}_{li} = \Phi_j/\Phi_i \tag{6.85}$$

Hence the maximum-likelihood estimate of $\boldsymbol{\beta}$ is obtained from

$$\hat{\beta}_i = \left[\sum_{j=1}^{k} \hat{\pi}_{lj}/\hat{\pi}_{li}\right]^{-1} \qquad (\text{for any } l \in [2, g]) \tag{6.86}$$

Thus the marginal budget shares are identifiable without further restrictions.

Next, we attempt to recover $\boldsymbol{\Theta}$, μ, and $\boldsymbol{\alpha}$ from the reduced-form coefficient matrix $\boldsymbol{\Pi}$. From (6.82), we equate $\boldsymbol{\Pi}_1$ with $\boldsymbol{\Theta} + \alpha_1\boldsymbol{\Phi}$. Keeping in mind that we have estimated $\boldsymbol{\beta}$, in terms of estimated entities this is,

$$\boldsymbol{\Theta} + \alpha_1\mu\hat{\boldsymbol{\beta}} = \hat{\boldsymbol{\Pi}}_1 \tag{6.87a}$$

which is a system of k equations involving $(k+2)$ unknowns; namely, k values of Θ_i, as well as μ and α_1. The identity

$$\mathbf{1}^T\boldsymbol{\Theta} \equiv (1-\mu)\boldsymbol{p}^T\boldsymbol{\gamma} \tag{6.87b}$$

might be considered an additional piece of information, except that it introduces the further unknown $\boldsymbol{p}^T\boldsymbol{\gamma}$. Besides $\sigma_w^2 = 0$, additional information is needed, apparently. If the permanent income generator is homogeneous ($\alpha_1 \equiv 0$) as

[41] Goldberger remarks that constraints of the type (6.77), $\sigma_w^2 \neq 0$, on the other hand, are not readily handled by orthodox econometric theory and software—Goldberger, "Maximum Likelihood Estimation . . .," op. cit. An algorithm for estimating a reduced form coefficient matrix subject to linear constraints operating on only part of it is given by Robert M. Hauser in "Disaggregating a Social-psychological Model of Educational Attainment," chapter 12 in A. S. Goldberger and O. D. Duncan, Eds., *Structural Equation Models in the Social Sciences* (New York: Seminar Press, 1973), pp. 255–284.

well as nonstochastic ($\sigma_w^2 = 0$), then it is clear from (6.87a) that $\boldsymbol{\Theta}$ is identified (and we would use that equation to estimate $\boldsymbol{\Theta}$).[42] This still falls short of complete identification: knowledge of $\boldsymbol{\Theta}$ and $\boldsymbol{\beta}$ does not serve to identify μ, γ and $\boldsymbol{\alpha}^\circ$. Apparently, this is because the marginal propensity to consume out of permanent income and permanent income come in observationally equivalent pairs $\{\mu, z\}$. In the model (6.69) with $\alpha_1 = 0$ and $w_t \equiv 0$, putting $\mu = \mu^\circ$ and $z = z^\circ$ generates identically the same distribution of the $\{v_{it}\}$ as does $\mu = \lambda\mu^\circ$, $z = \lambda^{-1}z^\circ$, where λ is any arbitrary scalar. Consequently, to fully identify the model it is necessary to normalize the permanent income measure by putting an arbitrary element of $\boldsymbol{\alpha}^\circ$ equal to a specific constant (say 1). Once this normalization has been made, the $\{\Phi_i\}$ are immediately identified as the elements in the corresponding row of $\boldsymbol{\Pi}$, and are estimated by the relevant $\{\hat{\pi}_{ij}\}$.

Given ML estimates of $\boldsymbol{\Phi}$ and $\boldsymbol{\Theta}$, an ML estimate of μ is obtained via (6.60). Given data on the fixed set of prices $\boldsymbol{p}$, an ML estimate of γ is obtained via (6.64).

6.2.5 Generation of Permanent Income Data: Some Options for Time Series.

The permanent income variable z_t consists of three parts: actual labor income y_t; nonlabor income (ρw_t); and the present value of expected future changes in labor income, $L_t(\dot{y})$. The last-mentioned variable is expectational, and the use of distributed lags (in one form or another) is the standard methodology for modelling it. Extrapolative (rather than adaptive) models seem called for in the projection of labor income gains (in nominal terms) into the future.[43]

Let $y_t(\tau)$ be the labor income expected to pertain in future period τ from the viewpoint of a decision-making consumer at actual time t. Historical labor income at t will be written y_t. Two simple options to describe expectations-formation behavior are, respectively, linear and exponential extrapolation:

$$y_t(\tau) = a_t + b_t(\tau - t) \tag{6.88}$$

$$\log[y_t(\tau)] = a_t + b_t(\tau - t) \tag{6.89}$$

If a_t and b_t are estimated by sliding least squares linear trend regressions consisting of t^* observations on $y_{t'}$ [or $\log y_{t'}$] regressed on a time index prior

---

[42] Putting $\alpha_1 = 0$ doesn't affect the rank either of $\boldsymbol{\Pi}$ or of $\boldsymbol{\Pi}_2$.

[43] For an individual consumer, life-cycle considerations would be a dominant superimposition. For the "representative consumer" of a stationary population, life-cycle effects may be assumed to cancel out in aggregation across the population.

to and including t, then explicit solutions for the above are

$$\hat{y}_t(\tau) = \hat{a}_t + \hat{b}_t(\tau - t)$$

$$= [W_1^T + (\tau + t^* - t) W_2^T] \, y_t^\circ \qquad (6.90a)$$

in which

$$W_1 = \frac{2(2t^* + 1)\mathbf{1} - 6j}{t^* - 1} \qquad (6.90b)$$

$$W_2 = \frac{6[2/(t^* + 1)j - \mathbf{1}]}{t^*(t^* - 1)} \qquad (6.90c)$$

with $\mathbf{1}$ a column of t^* units; j a vector containing the first t^* positive integers; and y_t° in the case of (6.88) is a vector containing t^* observations on labor income immediately before, and including, the observation y_t for period t. In the case of (6.89), y_t° contains observations on the logarithms of y_t.

The representation (6.90a, b, and c) of the extrapolative expectations hypothesis demonstrates clearly the nature of the distributed lag involved. The lag scheme has only one parameter, t^*; the weights attached to historic observations $y_{t-t^*+1}, y_{t-t^*+2}, \ldots, y_t$ decline monotonically as one proceeds from the present backwards through time. Weights sum to unity; unlike adaptive models, however, negative weights occur for the more remote past observations. Some empirical experience with the use of this lag scheme has been obtained with a series of experiments in which the ELES consumption function (6.58) was fitted using aggregative U.S. data.[44] As with other lag distributions there is no clear-cut procedure for an optimal choice of t^*. Maddala and Rao have recently revived the suggestion that $\bar{R}^2$ be used as a criterion to decide the trade-off between degrees of freedom lost by extending the length of a lag distribution against the better fit thereby obtained.[45] To implement this suggestion in the context of the estimation of ELES it would be necessary first to develop a suitable systems analogue of $\bar{R}^2$. The empirical evidence suggests that the serial properties of the residuals are influenced (sometimes markedly)

---

[44] Alan Powell, "An ELES Consumption Function for the United States," *Economic Record* 49, no. 127 (September 1973): 337–357.

[45] G. S. Maddala and A. S. Rao, "Maximum Likelihood Estimation of Solow's and Jorgenson's Distributed Lag Models," *Review of Economics and Statistics* 53, no. 1 (February 1971): 80–88.

by the length t^* of the finite lag distribution.[46] The value of some statistic such as the Durbin-Watson d or the first serial correlation coefficient of the residuals would need to be considered, probably, in the estimation of t^* from empirical data. But we are running too far ahead.

The purpose of the lag scheme is to generate values of $L_t(\dot{y})$. Using first differences as finite approximations to time derivatives, and keeping in mind that from the viewpoint of planning instant t, y_t is assumed known, we have from (6.90a),

$$\hat{\dot{y}}_t(\tau) = \hat{y}_t(\tau) - \hat{y}_t(\tau-1) \qquad (\text{for } \tau \geq t+2) \tag{6.91a}$$

$$= \hat{b}_t \qquad (\text{for } \tau \geq t+2) \tag{6.91b}$$

$$= \hat{y}_t(t+1) - y(t) \qquad (\text{for } \tau = t+1) \tag{6.91c}$$

Recall that ρ is the rate of discount to be used in forming the present value series $\{L_t(\dot{y})\}$. Abbreviating the notation somewhat, for the tth element of this series we have, from (6.91a, b, and c),

$$\hat{L}_t = \sum_{\tau'=1}^{\infty} (1+\rho)^{-\tau'} \hat{\dot{y}}_t(t+\tau') \tag{6.92}$$

$$= \hat{b}_t \sum_{\tau'=2}^{\infty} (1+\rho)^{-\tau'} + [\hat{a}_t + \hat{b}_t - y_t](1+\rho)^{-1} \tag{6.93}$$

$$\doteq \frac{\hat{b}_t}{\rho} \qquad [\text{provided } y_t \doteq \hat{a}_t]$$

We shall work with the linear extrapolative model.[47] Notice from (6.90a, b, and c) that

$$\hat{b}_t = W_2^T Q_t(y) \tag{6.94}$$

---

[46] The observation is based on empirical fits of ELES consumption functions using the extrapolative framework—at the date of writing, the only empirical systems application had been based on the assumption $L_t(\dot{y}) = 0$. See C. Lluch and R. Williams, "Consumer Demand Systems . . .," op. cit.; and C. Lluch and R. Williams, "Cross Country Demand and Savings Patterns: An Application of the Extended Linear Expenditure System," Development Research Center, World Bank, Washington, D.C., draft dated July 1973 (mimeo).

[47] A more detailed treatment of the linear extrapolative expectations model, and a treatment of the log linear case may be found in Alan Powell, "Estimation of Lluch's Extended Linear Expenditure System from Time-Series Data," paper read to the Third Conference of Economists (Economic Society of Australia and New Zealand), Adelaide, May 1973; available from Department of Economics, Monash University, Victoria 3168, Australia (mimeo).

in which Q_t is a truncation operator defined by

$$Q_t(y) \equiv y_t^{\circ} \tag{6.95}$$

The problem of determining t^* aside, the above procedure is made operational by substituting $(\hat{b}_t/\rho)$ for $L_t(\dot{y})$ in (6.28b), and then substituting from that equation into (6.48). We obtain

$$v_{it} = p_{it}\gamma_i + \mu\beta_i(Y_t - p_t^T\gamma) + \Psi_i\hat{b}_t + e_{it} \tag{6.96}$$

in which

$$\Psi_i = \beta_i(\delta/\rho^2) = \beta_i(\mu/\rho) \tag{6.97}$$

It may be that in some applications researchers will wish to estimate the rate of return on wealth ρ independently. In that case, the prior value of ρ would be used in conjunction with (6.93) and (6.28b) to generate a series on z_t; estimation would proceed using the (modified) Parks-Solari method on (6.48). An alternative would be to proceed as above, but varying ρ parametrically. The value of ρ giving the highest value of the likelihood function would (presumably) be selected; the time preference discount rate δ would then be estimated from (6.24).[48]

Although in (6.96) $\hat{b}_t$ is stochastic, it is a function of the labor income series, which is exogenous. In the microsetting, this is undoubtedly correct; however, most empirical exercises are likely to be based on available aggregative time-series data, and on the notion of the "representative consumer." Simultaneity bias due to the contemporaneous feedback of consumption on income determination could then be expected, at least for accounting periods of a year or more in length. A theoretical treatment of this problem remains to be developed.

---

[48] A commentator on a draft paper dealing with this problem correctly points out that it is quite ambitious to expect to obtain robust estimates of the capital-market parameter ρ, and of the pure rate of time preference, from consumer data. His opinion is confirmed by the author's experience in fitting the ELES consumption function to American data. See Powell, "An ELES Consumption Function for the U.S.A.," op. cit.

Bibliography

Allen, R. G. D. *Mathematical Analysis for Economists.* London: Macmillan, 1938.

Allen, R. G. D. *Mathematical Economics.* London: Macmillan, 1959.

Allen, R. G. D. "A Reconsideration of the Theory of Value." Part II. *Economica,* n.s., 1, no. 2 (May 1934): 196–219.

Arrow, K. J., H. B. Chenery, B. S. Minhas, and R. M. Solow. "Capital-Labor Substitution and Economic Efficiency." *Review of Economics and Statistics* 43 (August 1961): 225–250. Reprinted in Arnold Zellner, Ed. *Readings in Economic Statistics and Econometrics.* Boston: Little Brown 1968.

Bard, Y. "Nonlinear Parameter Estimation and Programming." I.B.M. Contributed Program Library 360D–13.6.003 (December 1967).

Barten, Anton P. "Consumer Demand Functions under Conditions of Almost Additive Preferences." *Econometrica* 32, no. 1–2 (January-April 1964): 1–38.

Barten, Anton P. "Estimating Demand Equations." *Econometrica* 36, no. 2 (April 1968): 213–251.

Barten, Anton P. "Maximum Likelihood Estimation of a Complete System of Demand Equations." *European Economic Review* 1, no. 1 (Fall 1969): 7–73.

Barten, Anton P. "Theorie en Empirie van een Volledig Stelsel van Vraagvergelijkingen." Ph.D. thesis, Netherlands School of Economics, 1966.

Basmann, R. L. "A Note on the Exact Finite Sample Frequency Functions of Generalized Classical Linear Estimators in Two Leading Overidentified Cases." *Journal of the American Statistical Association* 56, no. 295 (September 1961): 619–636.

Belandria, Francisco. "An Empirical Study of Consumer Expenditure Patterns in Venezuelan Cities." Ph.D. dissertation, North Western University, August 1971.

Brandow, G. E. "Interrelations Among Demand for Farm Food Products and Implications for Control of Market Supply." *Pennsylvania Experiment Station Bulletin* 680, 1961.

Bridge, J. L. *Applied Econometrics.* Amsterdam: North-Holland, 1971.

Brown, A., Richard Stone, and D. A. Rowe. "Demand Analysis and Projections for Britain, 1900–1970: A Study in Method." In J. Sandee, Ed. *Europe's Future Consumption,* vol. 2. Amsterdam: North-Holland, 1964. Pp. 200–225.

Brown, Murray, and Dale M. Heien. "The S-Branch Utility Tree: A Generalization of the Linear Expenditure System." *Econometrica* 40, no. 4

(July 1972): 737–747. Also available as Research Discussion Paper No. 1, Research Division, Office of Prices and Living Conditions, U.S. Bureau of Labor Statistics, Washington, D.C., 1972.

Byron, Ray P. "Methods for Estimating Demand Equations Using Prior Information: A Series of Experiments with Australian Data." *Australian Economic Papers* 7, no. 11 (December 1968): 227–248.

Campbell, Hugh G. *An Introduction to Matrices, Vectors and Linear Programming*. New York: Appleton-Century-Crofts, 1965.

Carlevaro, F., and E. Rossier. "Le Programme Linex pour l'Estimation des Parametres du Systeme Lineaire de Depenses." Faculté des Sciences Économiques et Socialies, Université de Genève, Centre d'Econometrie, Cahier, 15 June, 1970.

Christensen, Laurits Ray. "Saving and the Rate of Return." Ph.D. thesis, University of California, Berkeley, 1967. Available as Systems Formulation, Methodology and Policy Workshop Paper 6805, Social Systems Research Institute, University of Wisconsin, 1968.

Court, R. H. "Utility Maximization and the Demand for New Zealand Meats." *Econometrica* 35, no. 3–4 (July–October 1967): 424–446.

Dhrymes, Phoebus J. "On a Class of Utility and Production Functions Yielding Everywhere Differentiable Demand Functions." *Review of Economic Studies* 34, no. 4 (October 1967): 399–408.

Dhrymes, Phoebus J. *Econometrics: Statistical Foundations and Applications*. New York: Harper & Row, 1970.

Dhrymes, Phoebus J. "Equivalence of Iterative Aitken and Maximum Likelihood Estimators for a System of Regression Equations." *Australian Economic Papers* 10, no. 16 (June 1971): 20–24.

Dixon, Peter B. "The Theory of Joint Maximization." Ph.D. thesis, Department of Economics, Harvard University, April 1972.

Domar, E. "Recent Empirical Studies in the CES and Related Production Functions." In M. Brown, Ed. *The Theory and Empirical Analysis of Production*. New York: Columbia University Press, 1967 for N.B.E.R.

Ferguson, C. E., *The Neoclassical Theory of Production and Distribution*. Cambridge: Cambridge University Press, 1969.

Friedman, Milton. "Professor Pigou's Method for Measuring Elasticities of Demand from Budgetary Data." *Quarterly Journal of Economics* 50 (1935): 151–163.

Frisch, Ragnar. "A Complete Scheme for Computing All Direct and Cross Demand Elasticities in a Model with Many Sectors." *Econometrica* 27 (1959): 177–196.

Gamaletsos, Theodore. "Further Analysis of Cross Country Comparison of

Consumer Expenditure Patterns." *European Economic Review* 4, No. 1 (April 1973): 1–20.

Geary, R. C. "A Note on 'A Constant Utility Index of the Cost of Living.'" *Review of Economic Studies* 18 (1950–51): 65–66.

Goldberger, Arthur S. *Econometric Theory.* New York: Wiley, 1964.

Goldberger, Arthur S. "Functional Form and Utility: A Review of Consumer Demand Theory." University of Wisconsin, Systems Formulation, Methodology and Policy Workshop Paper 6703, October 1967.

Goldberger, Arthur S. "Maximum Likelihood Estimation of Regressions Containing Unobservable Independent Variables." *International Economic Review* 13, no. 1 (February 1972): 1–15.

Goldberger, Arthur S. "Multivariate Regression: A Descriptive Analysis." Social Systems Research Institute, University of Wisconsin, preliminary draft, November 1969 (mimeo).

Goldberger, Arthur S., and Theodore Gamaletsos. "A Cross-Country Comparison of Consumer Expenditure Patterns." *European Economic Review* 1, no. 3 (Spring 1970): 357–400.

Goldfeld, S. M., and R. E. Quandt. *Non-Linear Methods in Econometrics.* Amsterdam and London: North-Holland, 1972.

Goldman, S. M., and H. Uzawa. "A Note on Separability in Demand Analysis." *Econometrica* 32, no. 3 (July 1964): 387–398.

Gorman, W. M. "Separable Utility and Aggregation." *Econometrica* 27, no. 3 (July 1959): 469–481.

Hadar, Josef. *Mathematical Theory of Economic Behavior.* Reading, Mass.: Addison-Wesley, 1971.

Hadley, George. *Linear Algebra.* Reading, Mass.: Addison-Wesley, 1965.

Hauser, Robert M., "Disaggregating a Social-psychological Model of Educational Attainment." Chapter 12 in A. S. Goldberger and O. D. Duncan, Eds. *Structural Equation Models in the Social Sciences.* New York: Seminar Press, 1973, pp. 255–285.

Heien, Dale M. "Demographic Effects and the Multiperiod Consumption Function." *Journal of Political Economy* 80, no. 1 (January–February 1972): 125–138.

Henderson, J. M., and R. E. Quandt. *Microeconomic Theory.* New York: McGraw Hill, 1958.

Hicks, J. R. "A Reconsideration of the Theory of Value," Part I. *Economica* n.s. 1, no. 1 (February 1934): 52–76.

Hicks, J. R. *Value and Capital.* 2nd ed. Oxford: Clarendon Press, 1946.

Houthakker, H. S. "Additive Preferences." *Econometrica* 28, no. 2 (April 1960): 244–257.

Howe, Howard. "Preliminary Estimates of the Linear and Quadratic Expenditure Systems." University of Pennsylvania, Department of Economics, December 14, 1972 (mimeo).

Intriligator, Michael D. *Mathematical Optimization and Economic Theory*. Englewood Cliffs, N.J.: Prentice-Hall, 1971.

Johansen, Leif. "On the Relationships Between Some Systems of Demand Functions." University of Oslo, Institute of Economics, *Reprint Series* No. 47, Oslo, 1969. Reprinted from *Liiketaloudellinen Aikakauskirja*.

Klein, L. R., and H. Rubin. "A Constant Utility Index of the Cost of Living." *Review of Economic Studies* 15 (1948–49): 84–87.

Kmenta, Jan, and Roy F. Gilbert. "Small Sample Properties of Alternative Estimators of Seemingly Unrelated Regressions." *Journal of the American Statistical Association* 63, no. 324 (December 1968): 1180–1200.

Koopmans, T. C., H. Rubin, and R. B. Leipnik. "Measuring the Equation Systems of Dynamic Economics." In T. C. Koopmans, Ed. *Statistical Inference in Dynamic Economic Models*. New York: Wiley, 1950, Cowles Foundation Monograph No. 10, pp. 53–237.

Leser, C. E. V. "Commodity Group Expenditure Functions for the United Kingdom, 1948–57." *Econometrica* 29, no. 1 (January 1961): 24–32.

Leser, C. E. V. "Demand Functions for Nine Commodity Groups in Australia." *Australian Journal of Statistics* 2, no. 3 (November 1960): 102–113.

Leser, C. E. V. "The Pattern of Australian Demand." *Economic Record* 34 (1958): 212–222.

Lluch, Constantino. "Consumer Demand Functions, Spain, 1958–1964." *European Economic Review* 2, no. 3 (Spring 1971): 277–302.

Lluch, Constantino. "The Extended Linear Expenditure System." University of Essex Discussion Paper No. 16 (February 1970). A revised version has been published under the same title in *European Economic Review* 4, no. 1 (1973): 21–32.

Lluch, Constantino. "Systems of Demand Functions Under Intertemporal Utility Maximization." University of Essex, Department of Economics *Discussion Paper* no. 11, January 1970 (mimeo).

Lluch, Constantino, and Michio Morishima. "Demand for Commodities Under Uncertain Expectations." In M. Morishima, Ed. *Theory of Demand, Real and Monetary*, New York: Oxford University Press, 1973, ch. 5.

Lluch, Constantino, and Alan Powell. "International Comparisons of Expenditure and Saving Patterns." Development Research Center, World Bank, Washington, D.C., January 1973 (mimeo).

Lluch, Constantino, and Ross A. Williams. "Consumer Demand Systems and Aggregate Consumption in the U.S.A.: An Application of the Extended

Linear Expenditure System." Development Research Center, World Bank, Washington, D.C., May 1973 (mimeo).

Lluch, Constantino, and Ross A. Williams. "Cross Country Demand and Savings Patterns: An Application of the Extended Linear Expenditure System." Development Research Center, World Bank, Washington, D.C., July 1973 (mimeo).

Maddala, G. S., and A. S. Rao. "Maximum Likelihood Estimation of Solow's and Jorgenson's Distributed Lag Models." *Review of Economics and Statistics* 53, no. 1 (February 1971): 80–88.

Marquardt, Donald W. "An Algorithm for Least Squares Estimation of Non-Linear Parameters." *Journal of the Society of Industrial and Applied Mathematics* 11, no. 2 (1963): 431–441.

Modigliani, F., and R. Brumberg. "Utility Analysis and the Consumption Function: An Interpretation of Cross Section Data." In K. K. Kurihara, Ed. *Post Keynesian Economics*, New Brunswick: Rutgers University Press, 1954, pp. 388–436.

Parks, Richard W. "Maximum Likelihood Estimation of the Linear Expenditure System." *Journal of the American Statistical Association* 66, no. 336 (December 1971): 900–903.

Parks, Richard W. "Systems of Demand Equations: An Empirical Comparison of Alternative Functional Forms." *Econometrica* 37, no. 4 (October 1969): 629–650.

Pearce, I. F. *A Contribution to Demand Analysis*. New York: Oxford University Press, 1964.

Pearce, I. F. "An Exact Method of Consumer Demand Analysis." *Econometrica* 29, no. 4 (October 1961): 499–516.

Phlips, Louis. "A Dynamic Version of the Linear Expenditure Model." *Review of Economics and Statistics* 54, no. 4 (November 1972): 450–458.

Pigou, A. C. "A Method of Determining the Numerical Value of Elasticities of Demand." *Economic Journal* 20 (1910): 636–640.

Pollak, Robert A. "Additive Utility Functions and Linear Engel Curves." University of Pennsylvania, Department of Economics *Discussion Paper* No. 53, June 1967 (revised February 1968). Reprinted in *Review of Economic Studies* 38, no. 4 (October 1971): 401–414.

Pollak, Robert A. "Conditional Demand Functions and the Implications of Separable Utility." *Southern Economic Journal* 37, no. 4 (April 1971): 423–433.

Pollak, Robert A., and Terence J. Wales. "Estimation of the Linear Expenditure System." *Econometrica* 37, no. 4 (October 1969): 611–628.

Powell, Alan. "Aitken Estimators as a Tool in Allocating Predetermined

Aggregates." *Journal of the American Statistical Association* 64, no. 327 (September 1969): 913–922.

Powell, Alan. "The Analysis of Synoptic Cross-Section Data on Consumer Budgets." Development Research Center, World Bank, Washington, D.C., September 1972 (mimeo).

Powell, Alan. "A Complete System of Consumer Demand Equations for the Australian Economy Fitted by a Model of Additive Preferences." *Econometrica* 34, no. 3 (July 1966): 661–675.

Powell, Alan. "An ELES Consumption Function for the United States." *Economic Record* 49, no. 127 (September 1973): 337–357.

Powell, Alan. "Estimation of Lluch's Extended Linear Expenditure System from Cross Section Data." *Australian Journal of Statistics* 15, no. 2 (August 1973).

Powell, Alan. "Estimation of Lluch's Extended Linear Expenditure System from Time-Series Data." Paper read to the Third Conference of Economists (Economic Society of Australia and New Zealand), Adelaide, May 1973. Available from Department of Economics, Monash University, Victoria, Australia (mimeo).

Powell, Alan, Tran Van Hoa, and R. H. Wilson. "A Multi-Sectoral Analysis of Consumer Demand in the Post-War Period." *Southern Economic Journal* 35, no. 2 (October 1968): 109–120.

Ramsey, F. P. "A Mathematical Theory of Saving." *Economic Journal* 38, no. 152 (December 1928): 543–559.

Sampson, Gary P. "Productivity Change in Australian Manufacturing." Ph.D. dissertation, Department of Economics, Monash University, 1969.

Sato, Kazuo. "Additive Utility Functions with Double-Log Consumer Demand Functions." *Journal of Political Economy* 80, no. 1 (January–February 1972): 102–124.

Sato, Kazuo. "A Two-Level Constant Elasticity of Substitution Production *Review of Economic Studies* 34, no. 98 (April 1967): 201–218.

Solari, Luigi. "Sur L'Estimation du Systeme Lineaire de Depenses par La Methode du Maximum de Vraisemblance." Centre D'Econometrie, Cahier FN/5243.1/3, Faculté des Sciences Économiques et Sociales, Université de Genève, Mars 1969 (mimeo).

Solari, Luigi. *Theori des Choix et Fonctions de Consommation Semi-Agregées, Modeles Statistiques*. Geneva: Dros, 1971.

Stone, Richard. "Linear Expenditure Systems and Demand Analysis: An Application to the Pattern of British Demand." *Economic Journal* 64, no. 255 (September 1954): 511–527.

Stone, Richard. *Mathematical Models of the Economy and Other Essays*. London: Chapman and Hall, 1970.

Strotz, R. H. "The Utility Tree—A Correction and Further Appraisal." *Econometrica* 27, no. 3 (July 1959): 482–488.

Theil, Henri. *Economics and Information Theory*. Amsterdam: North-Holland and Chicago: Rand McNally, 1967.

Theil, Henri. "The Information Approach to Demand Analysis." *Econometrica* 33, no. 1 (January 1965): 67–87.

Tintner, Gerhard. "The Maximization of Utility over Time." *Econometrica* 6, no. 2 (1938): 154–158.

Tintner, Gerhard. "The Theoretical Derivation of Dynamic Demand Curves." *Econometrica* 6, no. 4 (1938): 375–380.

Weber, Warren E. "Interest Rates, Relative Prices, and Consumer Expenditures for Durables and Non-Durables: A Multiperiod Utility Maximization Approach." Department of Economics, Virginia Polytechnic Institute and State University, Blacksburg, Virginia, February 1972 (mimeo).

Yaari, Menahem E. "On the Consumer's Lifetime Allocation Process." *International Economic Review* 5, no. 3 (September 1964): 304–316.

Zaman, Arshad. "Formulation and Estimation of a Complete System of Demand Equations." Department of Economics, Michigan State University, *Econometrics Workshop Special Report No. 3*, September 1970.

Zellner, Arnold. "An Efficient Method of Estimating Seemingly Unrelated Regressions and Tests for Aggregation Bias." *Journal of the American Statistical Association* 57, no. 298 (June 1962): 348–368. Reprinted as *Reprint No. 27*, University of Wisconsin, Social Systems Research Institute, 1962.

Zellner, Arnold. "Estimation of Regression Relationships Containing Unobservable Independent Variables." *International Economic Review* 11 (October 1970): 441–454.

Index

About the Author

Alan A. Powell has been professor of econometrics at Monash University, Melbourne, Australia, since early 1968. During 1972, he was a visiting economist at the Development Research Center, World Bank, Washington, D.C. Previously he was a lecturer in economics at the University of Adelaide (1961–1964) and senior lecturer (later reader) in economics at Monash University (1965–1967). In 1964, he was post-doctoral fellow in political economy at the University of Chicago, and in 1968 he held, as a visiting Fullbright Fellow, an associate professorship at Rutgers University. Dr. Powell received the B.Sc.Agr. with honors in agricultural economics from the University of Sydney in 1959, and the Ph.D. at the same university in 1963. His research interests and published writings have been mainly in statistical applications to applied economic problems.